Advice Worth Ignoring: How Tuning Out the Experts Can Make You a Better Parent

"Dr. Ray is a voice of reason in what is often an unreasonable time. He makes us laugh, think, and reach for the best in us. He offers insight and hope for the daunting job of parenting with advice that takes into account our children's spiritual well-being, not just behavior modification. "

—ROSE MALAVOLTI, professional educator, speaker, and mother of twenty-one

"Dr. Ray dismantles all of the misguided ideas about parenting that flood our society today, and leaves you with commonsense wisdom that makes you feel calm, equipped, and excited to face your day as a parent. When you're done with this book, you'll feel as if a huge weight has been taken from your shoulders."

—JENNIFER FULWILER, radio host, bestselling author, and mom of six

Discipline That Lasts a Lifetime: The Best Gift You Can Give Your Kids

"Dr. Ray Guarendi's style of mixing humor with wise insights and sound advice for what to do and how to do it manages to be just that. Dr. Ray helps parents understand that discipline is an important way to love their children, and teaching them self-control is a gift that lasts a lifetime."

—PEG CARMACK SHORT, Editor-in-Chief, *Becoming Family Magazine*

"Dr. Ray deals with real-life questions and offers real-life answers. You'll find yourself saying, 'I can relate to that!'"

—Dan Seaborn, author, *26 Words That Will Improve the Way You Do Family*

"Dr. Ray has done it again! His list of snappy (but charitable) answers to rude questions is worth the price of the book. But there's so much more."

—Mike Aquilina, author, *Yours Is the Church*

"Dr. Ray gives practical spiritual advice while answering tough questions concerning raising children in the faith. A true guidebook of responses and actions to help parents and grandparents persevere in love while maintaining and passing on truth."

—Julie Dortch Cragon, author, *Amazing Graces: The Blessings of Sacramentals*

"This book is down to earth, practical, funny, and a breath of fresh air. Thanks Dr. Ray, from a father of nine!"

—Chris Padgett, coauthor, *Holy Marriage, Happy Marriage*

BEING A GRANDPARENT

BEING A GRANDPARENT

JUST LIKE BEING A PARENT...ONLY DIFFERENT!

DR. RAY GUARENDI

franciscan
media
Cincinnati, Ohio

Cover design by Paul Higdon
Book design by Mark Sullivan

LIBRARY OF CONGRESS CATALOGING-IN-PUBLICATION DATA
Names: Guarendi, Ray, author.
Title: Being a grandparent : just like being a parent only different /
Dr. Ray Guarendi.
Description: Cincinnati : Franciscan Media, 2018.
Identifiers: LCCN 2018001728 | ISBN 9781632532312 (trade paper)
Subjects: LCSH: Grandparent and child. | Grandparents. | Parenting.
Classification: LCC BF723.G68 G83 2018 | DDC 306.874/5—dc23
LC record available at https://lccn.loc.gov/2018001728

ISBN 978-1-63253-231-2

Published by Franciscan Media
28 W. Liberty St.
Cincinnati, OH 45202
www.FranciscanMedia.org

Printed in the United States of America
Printed on acid-free paper
19 20 21 22 5 4 3

Contents

INTRODUCTION

"Have you written a book for grandparents?" Up until now, I've had to answer, "Not yet." I have written books for parents, and the roles do overlap. The relationship generally holds: The better parent you were, the better grandparent you'll be.

The motives behind the question are diverse. Some first-time grandparents eagerly anticipate a new life-phase and plan to enter it with as much gusto as they entered parenthood. Some wonder how being a grandparent will differ from being a parent and want to mature into it with the fewest wrinkles. Some are a daily presence in their grandchildren's lives, often sharing a home with them and their parent(s) and wanting the contact to be as smooth as possible. Some are baffled as to why their own children are raising the grandkids so unlike they were raised—in practice, discipline, or morals. Others see their grandchildren as difficult to be around and ask what, if anything, they can do about it.

Helpless emotions pain those whose grandchildren have been removed from their lives. Because of family quarrels, in-law friction, or personality conflicts, Grandma or Grandpa are allowed little or no contact with the grandchildren. And they are desperate to find ways to rebuild the bridge.

All of these reasons and more have moved me to write a book for grandparents. As a beginning grandfather myself, I'm ready to learn from the experience of the veterans. I do know one thing for sure, though. I'm not about to be one of those who think, "My grandkid is the smartest, most adorable child to enter the northern hemisphere in the past century." My unofficial estimate is that 82.46% of grandparents think this about their first grandbaby. Still, in case you are at all interested, I can send you some videos. There's this really cute one of her spitting up strained peas. Would you prefer I email or text it? It's not that long.

Old Age Brings Youth or "I'm getting younger by the year."

I expected that I would enjoy being a grandparent. I underestimated how much.

"If I would have known grandkids were so much fun, I'd have had them first." This is a common sentiment. What makes being a grandparent so enjoyable for so many?

Grandchildren add youth. Enthusiasm, zest, energy—they have enough for themselves and us. We're getting older, but they're pulling on us to be younger. "Grandpa went on every ride with me, three times on the bumper cars." They give us a second go-around with kids. What we learned over decades of parenting, we can bring into their lives. We get some do-overs.

Grandchildren add love. The little ones especially see Grandma and Grandpa through adoring eyes. Few relationships are so unquestionably accepting. Who wouldn't revel in that kind of favor, especially if they had been raising teens not all that long ago.

Schedule flexibility. For most grandparents, the full-time demands of childrearing, maintaining a household and employment, if not gone, are passing. The structure of life is loosening, leaving more room for other priorities: "Mom, can you pick up Stanford from his Little College Preschool on Tuesdays?";

"Grandpa has come to every one of my games this year." Often, as many grandparents as parents are spectators. And most don't have to be elsewhere. They have time to linger, to celebrate victory or soothe defeat.

Financial latitude. "Grandma bought me this stuffed dog, and then she paid for two jumbo sundaes." Did you have that kind of financial freedom with your own children? And even if you did, were you restrained some by qualms about spoiling? Are you still as restrained? "Mom, please, no more stuffed animals. Eve's sleeping on the floor because they bury her bed, two layers deep." Many grandparents relish indulging more than they did as parents.

Declining discipline. Discipline is the hard work of parenthood, evoking a youngster's displeasure, however temporary, with his parents. Most grandparents left the authority role years back. Consequently, in the grandkids' eyes, they are just more agreeable and more attuned to childhood. "You didn't want to be mean, did you, Charity? You just felt bad because your brother's cookie had more chocolate chips than yours, huh?"

In any approval poll, which adult would rank higher? The one who took Charity's cookie because of her tantrum, or the one who wants to give her a different cookie with more chocolate chips?

Of course, if a grandparent in the pursuit of likeability regularly interferes with a parent's discipline, the kids will approve, but the parent will disapprove, a topic we'll address later.

Birth order effect. This is the drift toward a more relaxed—some might call it loose—parenting style with each additional child. My wife, Randi, and I have ten children. We prodded our oldest at age one to show off his knowledge of basic anatomy. "Where are your eyes? Where's your nose? Where's your vagus nerve?" Our youngest was eight when I thought to ask her, "Can you count?" When Peter, our ninth, was about three months old, someone asked Randi, "Is Petey sleeping through the night yet?" She wryly answered, "I don't know if he is, but we are." Birth order mellows parents and grandparents alike.

The very same behavior from me that upset my father, he somehow found excusable, even cute, from my own children. It took more childish misconduct to frustrate him. As one comedian observed, "These are not the same people who raised us. These are older people trying to get into heaven."

The birth order effect can reemerge with grandchildren. My parents saw the arrival of eighteen grandchildren in twenty years. Mom wallpapered her family room with pictures of grandkids one through ten. She stuck kid-drawn stick figures of the last eight to her refrigerator. They were in color, though.

Grandkids, their love, life's flexibility, birth order mellowing—it all adds up to the chance to smell more roses and fewer diapers.

So why didn't you have the grandchildren first?

Dealing with Distance or "They live too far away."

My daughter, husband, and their three children (ages eight, twelve, fourteen) relocated to another state due to a job transfer. We miss them badly. Any tips for out-of-state grandparents?

Growing up I had five pairs of aunts and uncles, two grandfathers, and a grandmother, all living within a five-mile radius. When I was four, my family moved some seven miles from my grandparents. Being Italian, I wondered if we were breaking some kind of rule.

Italian or not, for most of history, generations lived geographically close, relying upon each other. Grandparents were connected to the whole family, giving guidance from experience.

These days, families are separated, some would say scattered, around the country, the world even. For the older, retirement can bring freedom of relocation not possible in earlier years. For the younger, careers can demand uprooting, often more than once. One survey reported that the typical family moves about every four years.

While modern living is putting more miles between more families, it also is providing ways to shorten those miles. It is allowing travel by technology.

In college my main link to home was a letter sent by snail mail. Contrary to my grandchildren's belief, the Pony Express was no longer an option. Phones had been invented, but with long-distance charges slightly less than tuition, calls were few and short. By current measure, communication was slow and effortful.

For better and worse, today's youth are enamored with ease and speed—texts, Skype, email, instant messaging (Is instant fast enough?), Face Page, Space Book, or whatever they're called. As a last resort, a few will even leave a voice message.

Most of us seniors are aware of the latest communication options. We just may be freshmen at navigating them. A popular internet picture shows a two-year-old child on a cell phone, hand to his head in frustration, repeating, "No, Grandma, right-double-click on the icon."

While we may be competent with what we grew up with, the younger set is competent with what they're growing up with. It's what they use. Get familiar with how they use it. Use it yourself, even if not as easily as they do.

Technology, no matter how sophisticated, can never replace the personal, but it does provide an ever-ready entrance into a loved one's world. As a nod to your own youth, you could still write a letter. Just Google "form letters for grandparents."

When communication travels at the speed of light (186,000 miles per second), distance shrinks. Still, you're not there. On a moment's notice, you can't catch Babe's baseball game or babysit Storm fifteen minutes after being called. Your visits are planned. They are special events. Therefore, special events mean gifts. In other words, the temptation is to use more presents to compensate for less presence. However well-intentioned, this can backfire. It can teach the kids to value what you bring instead of who you are.

As a guideline, give gifts as you would if you lived next door, assuming, of course you wouldn't overdo it from next door. Birthdays, baptisms, graduations, and weddings are natural for gift-giving. Columbus Day and Ground Hog Day are not. Consider a hotel. When your children lived nearby, you probably seldom stayed overnight. Now that states separate you, your visits are fewer but longer. Ben Franklin warned, "Fish and visitors smell after three days." You're not a visitor; you're family, and you bathe regularly. So why a hotel? It's not an obligation; it's an option. It's an invitation to give the family, and you, a little private time.

What if you don't mention a Motel 6, but your children do? Don't take it personally, as in, "We're not here all that often, so you'd think we'd be welcome to stay a few nights." Because you're family doesn't mean your continuous presence might not add a few wrinkles to their family routine.

What if neither spouse will hear of you leaving? Don't debate. You've got a unanimous vote to stay, assuming your spouse votes likewise.

What if one parent insists you stay, and the other stays mute, or searches the internet for all accommodations within twenty-five miles? Unless both are of one voice, accept the hotels printout. The grandkids may vote for your staying, but they're not yet voting age.

Above all, day or night, be on your very best behavior. Be pleasant, helpful, easygoing. Keep opinions to yourself unless asked. Don't dwell on any drama back home. In other words, be as likeable as you can be. The warm afterglow will stretch across visits.

One last suggestion: If you do stay, make your bed and hang up your wet towel. You wouldn't have to do that at a hotel, you know.

Out of State, Out of Mind? or "I don't feel like I'm part of their lives."

We live several hundred miles from my son and his family. His in-laws live in their city and are a regular presence in the grandkids' lives. Sometimes we feel like the faraway, almost forgotten grandparents.

We've just talked of ways to raise your profile as a grandparent when miles conspire to lower it. In sum, travel via speed of light communications and visit via video.

With all that, geographically speaking, you are the more distant grandparents. That is the reality that confronts you. You can't be in the seats at most activities, watch a child on a half-hour notice, or drive anyone anywhere regularly. The everyday cycle of their family life is something you generally hear about. It's understandable, then, to wonder if your profile is slipping some. Distance can cause frustration.

Someone somewhere once said, "Frustration is the gap between the way things are and the way we want them to be." To lower the frustration, close the gap. There are two ways to do this: One, alter your reality, or two, alter your thinking.

To alter your reality, you could relocate to their city, perhaps the same block. Or persuade them to relocate near you. If that's not feasible, desirable even, you are left with altering your thinking. Such is likely easier than moving.

Here's a realistic thought: Modern families are spreading all over the map. In my own family, three of our children are out of state, with more possibly heading in that direction. (Am I the common denominator?) My daughter and her husband have the gall to live several hundred miles away, along with our first granddaughter. I've asked, "Couldn't you have moved after we had a few other grandkids?" They've replied, "I don't think the army would agree." One consolation for us is that the other grandparents live over 1,500 miles from them. Relatively speaking, we are the nearby grandparents.

Like us, you are forced to accept the reality of families in motion. The more you can, the less frustration you'll feel at the separation.

Reality thought: Distance won't automatically move you from a child's mind. True, the other grandparents are present more, but your presence is anticipated. Kids like parties, and Grandma and Grandpa's visits are party-like. Special activities, outings, ice cream with every breakfast (but only after finishing your cookie). "When are Grandpa and Grandma coming again?" can linger between visits.

Reality thought: Presence is not the sole element of a connection. What happens during that connection tightens or loosens it. Are you affectionate, kind, playful? If these mark your periodic presence, they will mark you.

Have you ever heard someone say, "I hadn't seen my friend since she moved away two years ago. We got together last week and picked up right where we left off. It was like she never left"? When you revisit your family after several months, you pick up right where you left off. It's like you never left.

I'm not diminishing the value of presence. I'm saying that less presence doesn't equate to forgotten presence. Each of your visits can resurrect all the reasons why the out-of-state grandparents are neat people. At least that's what I'm aiming for with my first granddaughter.

Just in case, though, I always pick up the restaurant check. That should add value to our visits.

Absence Makes the Heart Grow Calmer or "It may be better not to see each other too often."

My son's family lives several hours from us, making our visits infrequent. Given the troubles in our relationship, I can't help but think the distance is good, but I want to get along better when we do see them.

Distance may be an adversary when family ties are tight. It can be an ally when they're loose. Time between visits can settle irritations and ill feelings. Using the lingo of kids' games, it can make for a better do-over.

Here are some suggestions for better do-overs.

You can get along with—endure?—almost anyone if your time with them has a clear end in sight. After all, in three days, you'll be leaving for home. Actually, it's three days, six hours, and twenty-four minutes, but who's counting?

Christmas Eve is not the goodwill gathering you'd hope. Nonetheless, the get-together starts around 6 p.m. and tapers off by 10 p.m. That's only four hours you have to control your emotions and discipline your tongue. You can do that. You can be sociable, pleasant even—fake it if necessary—when your contact is measured in short stretches, be it hours or days.

Realize that you could be viewed as the more difficult one.

Whether you actually are or not is irrelevant. That's the perception. When families have friction, commonly each party sees the other as the main source. It's human nature. We want to believe ourselves more agreeable than the average bear, certainly more agreeable than those we find disagreeable.

It is humbling to think that after trying for so long to be cordial, not only could you be getting little credit for your effort, but you are seen as the one needing to show more effort. There is one thought more humbling: You might need more effort.

Suppose after a particularly rocky visit, you scrutinize yourself. You admit that you have a share in the troubles, if only 25% worth. Sometimes you overreact or become opinionated. Therefore, work on your 25%. Apologize for your share, whenever and however. In so doing, you may get the other to look at her 75%. The surest way to change another is to change oneself.

Resist Retaliation. For most of us most of the time, this means through words. Curb the urge to "set her straight" or to "let him know exactly how I feel." Have you done so in the past? Did it clear the air or cloud it? If you find another person difficult, remember: Difficult people don't see themselves as difficult. If they did, they wouldn't be so difficult.

Don't return verbal fire with fire. The danger of a simple disagreement spiraling out of control will drop dramatically. Also, you won't have to apologize later for your 25% share of the trouble. If you must vent, vent on the ride home with your spouse. Will several hours on the road be long enough? Take the back roads.

Exercise plan B: A hotel stay. A good choice when visits are smooth, it is better when visits have bumps. Absent a personalized, written invite to "stay here tonight," look to sleep elsewhere. Should your hosts present the idea first, try not to be offended. If you feel uncomfortable during the day, assume they do, too. A night of decompression can make tomorrow more inviting. On the other hand, if you're asked to stay, don't debate. Assume it's genuine. Even if you have doubts, there's always tomorrow night.

Getting along better with someone often means getting along less poorly. If that someone is the irascible neighbor two doors down, your contact is a smile and a honk as you drive on. If that someone is family, it is in your utmost interests to make your contacts as agreeable as possible. Remind yourself: That family member is the parent of your grandchildren.

Watch Where You Sit or "My grandchildren are not easy for me to watch."

I would be more enthused about watching my grandchildren for my son and his wife, but they aren't so easy to watch.

"Aren't so easy to watch." Is that a soft way to say the kids can be unruly and uncooperative? In other words, they don't listen. If so, yours is a common reason why a grandparent may be less willing to watch their grandchildren and may routinely hide behind a sudden bout of sinusitis.

How can you become more willing? Three strategies.

1) Tell your son and his wife you'll watch Conan and Storm under certain conditions. One, if they're asleep when you arrive and stay that way until you're gone. Two, if they will act nicer, like your other grandchildren. Three, if you can hire a security guard to sit with you.

2) Take a video of the kids' conduct for later viewing with their parents. Pause during ugly scenes to add your commentary.

3) Admit that you're not the disciplinarian you once were—whether true or not. As such, you're open to ideas on how to better handle the kids.

Strategy one is your first choice if you'd rather never watch Conan or Storm again. It is almost guaranteed to evoke excuses, disagreements, or defensiveness. Even if Mom and Dad realize there is truth to what you're implying, they won't be ready to admit it. Few parents want to hear how bad their kid is. Strategy one would remove you from any future sitting. The relationship cost would be high, though. Let this one sit.

Strategy number two does provide visual backup to your reports. The images are worth thousands of words. Nonetheless, if parents are slow to hear about how bad their child is, they may be even slower to want to see it. Again, not an approach that's good for your relationship. Besides, do you want your expensive video equipment anywhere near Conan?

Strategy number three is your only good option. While it might bruise your self-image—in fact, you are every bit the competent disciplinarian you once were—it has the most potential to get parental cooperation. By taking most of the focus off the kids and putting it on you, you're asking for help rather than saying, "Your kids are too hard to watch."

It also has the best chance to get Mom and Dad to ask, "How were the kids?" If they do, don't hedge. "Oh, for the most part they were okay," or "I forgot how much energy kids have." Be diplomatic, but be specific. "Tiger wouldn't stop hitting golf balls against the wall until I gathered them up." Then ask, "What would you like me to do if this happens next time?"

If neither parent asks, you can ask, "Do you want to know how the kids were?" Mix in some good with the bad. Make up the good if you have to.

At one time, our ten children were all under age thirteen. The prevailing union rate for watching that number was $32.00 per hour, plus a matching 401(k). Mom and Pop were our sitter saviors, so we learned quickly to ask about the kids' behavior. If we didn't ask, Mom gave us a look, saying, "Don't you have something to ask us?"

Looking back, I've done some calculations. My parents saved us around $21,000 in sitter fees. To repay them, I took them out to dinner. It was a really nice place. Though Mom gave me her look throughout the whole meal.

You can ask the parents before they leave, "What would you like me to do if _____?" Hopefully, they won't answer, "Oh, Joy would never do that." If they do, say, "Well, just in case, I'd like to know how to handle it best." This might also signal Mom or Dad to forewarn little Joy to behave.

Worst case scenario: Despite your best efforts, the kids and parents are slow to cooperate. Now you are facing a hard question: Can I enjoy my grandchildren if my disciplinary hands are tied? Some grandparents say yes. Their time with the kids is worth more to them than whatever unpleasantness occurs. Some say no. The unruliness makes the kids too hard to enjoy. Only you can decide where your personal balance is.

Time usually alters the scenario. That is, the kids either act better over time or worse. The parents take a firmer stance with the kids or they don't. If things do get unmanageable, you may have to be frank with your son and his wife. You want to be with the kids, but you need more cooperation. As a volunteer you have the main voice in your sitting conditions.

Is that your sinusitis acting up again?

Your Children, My House or "Shouldn't I be able to discipline the kids when they're with me?"

I watch my two grandchildren, ages five and nine, after school in my house. Doesn't being in my home allow me to discipline my way?

There are three possible scenarios here. One, you and their parents agree on your authority. Two, you don't agree; they think you discipline poorly or too much. Three, you don't agree; they think you discipline too little or are too permissive.

Scenario one is optimal for all, older and younger. When both generations are of one disciplinary voice, the kids are better behaved, the grandparents are happier, and the parents don't have to find other help. What you expect—in respect, cooperation, schedule, sibling harmony—will be more enforceable when the parents acknowledge you have the right to expect it. Put another way, everybody agrees: It's your house and your rules.

When a parent regularly asks how the kids behaved, that's even better. If Leonardo knows that his slightest of transgressions—say, spray-painting his name on the garage door—within a few hours will come to parent awareness, he'll think twice about displaying his artwork, at least where it's so visible.

Even when asked, my mother and father were sometimes slow

to describe how the kids behaved for them, preferring to paint a quasi-Hallmark picture. No matter. We would hear the gritty details from one or more of our daughters—who did what to whom, when and how much—all before we backed out of the driveway, and all about their brothers.

"Dad, want to hear what Sammy did while we were eating? I took notes."

Supporting my parents was a must. First, they deserved the kids' respect and cooperation. Our oversight went a long way to ensure that. Second, Mom and Pop were always willing to help for free. And they fed the kids, too.

Scenario two: You and the parents don't agree about discipline. They think your way is too old-fashioned. They want you to discipline as they do.

You don't see your way as heavy-handed. In fact, your hand has gotten lighter with the years. Still, the difference between how you'd like to handle trouble and how the parents would like you to is a source of discussion, at the least, or conflict, at the worst.

On one hand, it is your house, and you are the adult present. That gives you some measure of authority. On the other hand, it is their child and their discipline preference. That gives them natural authority. So where is the meeting ground?

Begin by establishing what you can do. Does Mom or Dad spank? If no, then you can't. And if yes, they might want no one else to spank, even Grandma. Can you send Harmony to the corner? No, they think the corner is demeaning. Is sitting on the couch or steps OK? Yes, but no longer than one minute per year of age. Can you assign Edgar Allen to write sentences as discipline?

What privileges can you remove? Find out the parameters. In the extreme, you are only to discipline as the parents would, which in your opinion is not much.

Next, decide what you can live with or, as it were, sit with.

Will Mom's sticker reward chart work in your house? Their approach is not yours, but, all things considered, can you live with compromise? Bigger stickers might do it, maybe Scratch 'n Sniff?

Certain misconduct you may have to prohibit and discipline regardless of the parents' guidelines. Physical aggression, disrespect, assaults on your house are on your nonnegotiable list. It is one thing to live within the discipline parameters set by the parents. It is quite another for you or your house to be mistreated. Every grandparent has the right to set his or her personal tolerance limits.

An irony: If your kids believe your discipline raised them well, why is it so questionable with their kids?

Scenario three: Mom and Dad believe you are too slow to discipline. One consolation might be that the grandkids disagree. They think you are plenty quick enough, thank you.

Here, it is wise to respect your children's discipline standards, even if you believe they are too strict or overprotective or out of step with most parents. Since they are the parents, they have wide leeway in how they raise their kids. In short, they have the right to be wrong.

Should you try to compensate for what you see as the parents' overly tight conditions regarding food, or computer, or TV, or bedtime, you risk undercutting the parents and potentially risk losing preferred sitter status. Parents have curtailed Grandma and/or Grandpa's grandkid time because they refused to abide by their wishes (more on this later). Don't force your kids into making that choice.

Maybe you'd like your own children to read my answer to your question. You have two alternatives. One, buy this book for them. Two, copy these pages and hide them in your grandchild's school book.

My House, My Discipline? or "The kids act up at my house, and their parents just watch."

When my grandchildren visit, they misbehave—lots. Their parents mostly either don't notice or allow it. I'm unsure what I can do about it.

What you can do about it would depend upon: (1) what exactly the kids are doing and, (2) what exactly their parents are doing about it.

What exactly are the kids doing? Do they defy Mom or Dad? Demand? Argue? Disrespect? In other words, do the kids mistreat their parents? That can get real ugly real fast; nonetheless, it involves the children and their parents. You are in effect a bystander, a witness. You could roll your eyes, but probably that too would either go unnoticed or be seen as a silent scold. Better to keep your looks to yourself.

Same with exasperated sighs. Work to master inscrutable, Buddha-like impassivity. Watch, but don't speak.

When I witness a relative or friend being ill-treated by his or her child, my mind fills with instruction, but that's where it stays. For one thing, people are paranoid around psychologists. ("Are you analyzing me?") For another, nobody is asking my guidance or paying me for it. Should they ask, I hand them a form, "Would you sign this, please? It gives me written permission to speak, in case I say something you don't want to hear." All right, not always. Sometimes I just have them initial it.

If you're at all like me, staying silent is a challenge. It's hard to watch kids behaving with impunity. It's not good for the kids or their parents. Still, when does the scenario become your business?

When the misconduct is toward you. When the disrespect or nastiness directly affects you. Then, no matter the parent's obliviousness or permissiveness, you have a legitimate right to defend yourself and speak up. Speaking up, however, may be your limit. Any discipline may be off-limits. Because of practicalities or parental push-back, you may not be able to place any consequences on the behavior. Your hope is to make Mom or Dad mindful of what is happening before their eyes. Avoid a tone of, "Will you do something with this child?" That may be your thought, but the words risk confrontation.

Why is this risky? If Rip's parents saw his behavior as all that discipline-worthy, they likely would act or at least warn him. That they don't is a sign they don't think it's as much of a problem as you do.

What if Rip is assaulting your house or its parts? Again, if no other big person moves to stop him, you have every right to.

As a child, when my exploratory instincts pushed me to roam into the bedrooms or workroom of my grandmother's house, she stopped me. She didn't wait for my parents to act. If my mother was occupied feeding my younger sister and my father was asleep, I made my move. Grandma, we were convinced, never slept.

Since it's your house, you have owner's rights to set terms for its treatment. As one friend curtly told a relative while his children stomped through her plants, "How they treat your flowers is up to you. How they treat mine is up to me."

What if Butkus and Bruno are not doing anything objectionable to their parents, you, or your house? Their hostility is aimed at each other. If the parents are oblivious, try a roundabout remark: "I hope nobody gets hurt," or "They can treat each other mean, can't they?" Without really saying so, you are saying, "Are you going to do something?" If nothing else, you're nudging Mom or Dad into awareness. If they're aware but still permissive, your comments may not register. Again, unless someone truly is in harm's way—that is, Chuck is flinging shoes at Aimee—the battle involves them and their parents. You can, however, step in to protect your furniture from his errant throws.

Is all this to say that a grandparent's role to discipline is limited, even in his or her own home? When the parents are present, yes. It becomes a matter of who is doing what to whom, when, and where. When you are the whom, and your house is the where, then you can rightly speak up, and if need be, act on the what.

Too Tired to Sit or "I can't watch the kids as much as I'm asked."

I enjoy watching my grandchildren, ages four and seven. Sometimes, though, I'm asked more than I'm able or willing.

Grandparents are first-line sitters. One reason is geography. Living near their children, they are available and can jockey their schedule, often on short notice.

Another reason is economic. Grandparents sit gratis, unlike the neighbor teen, who charges twenty bucks an hour plus benefits. Though a few grandparents do confess, "They couldn't pay me enough to do what I'm doing for free."

Connecting is a third reason. Sitting is one-to-one, a "Just me and you, huh, Grandma?" bond. The time is high value, even if Grandpa dozes off on the recliner two hours before the four-year-old's bedtime.

Love is the overarching reason. The attachment to one's grandchildren can be intense. Many grandparents didn't anticipate how strong it would be. Pictures alone provide strong testaments. Star's portfolio dwarfs that of all Grandma's own children combined, and she just turned three.

"I'm asked more than I'm able or willing." Can I assume you are older now than you've ever been? And that you might have lost a step or two since your own parenting days? My wife and I, nearing the close of thirty years of childrearing, watch young parents and wonder, "Did we have that much energy once?" Neither of us clearly remembers.

"Headlights and taillights" is one grandmother's pithy summary of her grandsons' visits. Headlights beamed arrival; let the action begin. Taillights signaled departure; let the recovery begin. As much as she enjoyed those boys, she knew her stamina was a fraction of theirs, and she didn't want fatigue or frustration—hers—to mar their visit. To borrow a line from a popular movie detective, "A grandma's got to know her limitations."

Even if stamina doesn't limit your sitting, your schedule might. Though others may not see that playing a role. "Now that you're retired, how do you fill your days? It must be pretty quiet with no kids left at home." (What's to say they won't boomerang back?) Translation: "Your time is now far more flexible." Perhaps, but it may not be as flexible as it appears.

While former obligations are gone, others have taken their place. When you were raising your kids, they gathered in one place: your house. Now that they've scattered, staying connected is more complicated. A standard retiree mantra is: "How did I get everything done when I worked full time?" Someone, including a close family member, looking at you from the outside may not understand why you don't have the flexibility he thinks naturally arrives with the passing of hands-on parenting and career.

What if your energy and time are able, but you're not always willing? Does that make you "ungrandparent-like?" Unaccommodating? Accommodation doesn't equate to a yes every time you're asked. Only you can decide what you're in a position to do, when, where, and how often. When considering availability, desire is a legitimate factor.

"I feel like I'm being taken advantage of." This might be risky to say to your child. One reaction, spoken or unspoken, could be resentment, "See if I ask you anymore." It's better to give reasons related to time and stamina.

"I just don't have the energy I used to. That day (week) is absolutely jammed. I don't think I could add anything else to it." These are legitimate explanations. You're not dodging or trotting out flimsy excuses. These are realities, are they not?

Once more, you are neither a lax nor neglectful grandparent because your idea of reasonable sitting help is less than your children's. When you were raising them, you had to make decisions they didn't agree with. Sometimes that still happens.

I would watch my grandkids more, but my bedtime is earlier than theirs, and my afternoon nap is longer.

Grandma vs. the Experts or "I think I learned a thing or two about raising children."

I don't recall questioning my parenting like parents do these days. My daughter has more self-doubts raising her six-year-old son than we did with all five of our children. What's changed?

A whole lot. Too many to elaborate here, but two stand out: society and me.

Society. Throughout history, societies changed ever so imperceptibly. Their structure, beliefs, morals, if they did shift, did so over many decades. Consequently, from one generation to the next, the social milieu in which children were raised stayed predictably constant.

Accelerating technology, for better and worse, has transformed all that, putting societal change on fast-forward. Parents face a landscape far more complex and challenging to navigate. Put simply, it's just not as easy to raise a child today than one single generation ago.

Twelve years separate our oldest from our youngest—a time span equal to a half generation. Our oldest spent the first half of childhood without the presence of such things as computers, smart phones, and morally decayed pop culture. Our youngest began life with these everywhere. No question, raising her raised more questions for us than raising her oldest brother. What's the second big change? People like me. Meaning, the childrearing professionals. Waves of new and improved notions for guaranteeing well-adjusted children have swamped parents. Not that all are useless or misleading, but their net effect has produced a level of parental insecurity and self-doubt not seen in past generations.

"Psychological correctness" is the label I've given to this widespread childrearing phenomenon. It is the idea that there are psychologically correct ways to teach and communicate discipline; in short, raise an emotionally stable youngster. What's more, deviating from these ways comes with dire social and psychological repercussions. No wonder parents tread so nervously. They wonder if they're applying the right formulas.

When some of the formulas don't work, they're befuddled. "What's wrong? Why am I not seeing success?" This leads to more self-questioning, insecurity, and searching for newer and better techniques.

How can a grandparent counter all this? First, don't get pulled into the pace of the culture. Make sure that whatever your activities and gifts are, particularly of a digital kind, they meet parental approval. If your daughter feels beleaguered by a society pulling her son through childhood years too soon, don't align with society. Align with your daughter.

Parents tell me of grandparents buying the kids televisions, computer games, cell phones, and cars that even the parents don't want and wouldn't buy. Don't make your daughter choose between her motherhood and her mother's (or father's) wishes.

What about those experts whose ideas are directing your

daughter? If she wants their direction, that's her prerogative. She sees their way as the better way, an improvement from the past, even though she doesn't see how it is fueling her insecurity.

On the other hand, if her self-doubt is building along with her frustration, your advice may be a relief. Help her to assess the problem: What do you see as the differences between my parenting and yours? Where do you disagree with what I did? Are you rethinking your discipline? Did we have more or less authority than you do? Which expert advice do you think clashes most with your instincts and common sense? Do the experts agree with your beliefs about life and morals?

With time, many parents reassess the worth of the ideas guiding them. If your daughter is one of them, you may just be the expert she turns to.

Jekyll and Hyde Grandchildren or "The kids behave fine for me."

My son and daughter-in-law struggle with disciplining their children, ages seven and three. When the kids are with me, though, I don't have much trouble with them.

There are several possible explanations for this. One, you discipline better than they do. You've been a parent a lot longer, with a discipline style forged in the childrearing trenches. You know what works, how, and when. Consequently, the grandkids don't race at you like they do at their parents. They know your speed limit is lower.

Kids and guard dogs have traits in common. This isn't meant as a slam on guard dogs, who are easier to toilet train and generally more obedient. Sensing insecurity makes a guard dog more bold. Sensing insecurity makes a kid more bold. If your demeanor is quietly in charge, young Oxford and Felicity can sense that and act accordingly.

Many parents sit stunned in parent-teacher conferences after hearing, "I just love having your son (daughter) in class. He's a delight. I'd take a whole class of him." Whereupon, the folks gape at each other in disbelief, pull out a recent photo and ask, "Is this the child? A brown-haired boy with freckles? Do I have the right room? Who are you? What school is this?"

A child's conduct depends much upon where he is, what the rules are, what grown-ups are present, and how much authority he perceives they have. A strong-willed child with one person may be nothing of the sort with another person.

Explanation number two: Familiarity may not always breed contempt, as the adage asserts, but it does breed familiarity. The kids have lived with their parents for years, more than enough time to figure out their disciplinary ways. If they're more talk than action, the kids know that. If they discipline only when they've had enough, they know that, too. In short, they can read their parents, even the three-year-old who can't read yet. But he can look at the picture.

Explanation number three. Your discipline is looser than theirs. As they might put it, "You don't have as much trouble with the kids because you let them get away with a lot more." A simple disciplinary formula: The more yielding one is, the less opposition she receives. "Now, Candy, you know you have to finish your cookie before you get ice cream. That's Grandpa's rule."

A warning: To enjoy being with the kids as they get older, you will have to be less loose and more firm, even if doing so runs counter to your preference.

Let's assume explanation number one: You don't have problems with the kids because you discipline well. As I've cautioned elsewhere, don't hold that over Mom and Dad. It sounds superior and is unlikely to receive a comment such as, "You're right. I've been noticing for some time now how much more competent you are with the kids than I am. Would you be willing to give me some tips?"

Many parents are frustrated with their disciplinary practices but aren't sure why. They're trying to do all the psychologically up-to-date things, while their parents follow the old ways and seem to be having more success. Why this is so might be something Mom and Dad would best come to realize on their own. Then they'll ask for those tips.

"They were good until you got here." The sight of her parents becomes Chastity's signal to amplify her unruliness. Nonetheless, the sight of her parent becomes your signal to step back and assume observer status. No matter how strong your impulse to correct—child or parent—be cautious. Until Mom and Dad notice the difference between your discipline and theirs, and until they ask you for your opinion, let them do their own disciplining.

If asked, "How were the kids for you?" be forthright. "They always behave pretty well for me." Whereupon, you'll get the same deer-stare that parents give to teachers, and you'll hear, "Who are you? You look like my mother."

"Mom (Dad), why don't they push you like they push me?" This is the question you want to hear. Be supportive and affirming. "Because your discipline isn't very good." OK, check that. Try, "Why do you think that is?" A basic psychology tactic: Answer a question with a question. You're nudging the parent toward self-scrutiny.

In the meantime, should the parents show little inclination to figure out why the kids are better behaved for you (Do they even know that?), you still benefit. The kids are pleasant with you, which makes it that much easier for you to be pleasant with them.

My Kid Doesn't Listen or "Why don't they follow the advice they're asking for?"

My daughter comes to me frustrated with her children's behavior. She asks for my advice, but then she either ignores it or argues with it.

Not all who seek my counsel want it. They seek my agreement with their own self-counsel. To guarantee someone would like my advice, I'd need to figure out what he wants to hear and then say it.

What is your daughter seeking: empathy or guidance? Empathy may help her feel better for the meantime. Good guidance will do more to ease her building frustration.

"I've tried that. It doesn't work," say the parents. Exploring why, I hear similar themes: inconsistency, poor perseverance, shaky follow-through, fatigue, spouses who disagree. Having talked with hundreds of parents, I've learned ways to move past resistance. Since you probably don't have hundreds of children, you might be unsure how to respond to your daughter's resistance.

Rather than answering her every objection, begin with a question. "Do you like living with so much frustration?" She'll probably give you a look that says, "What kind of question is that?" Press on, "Is what you're doing working?" Again an unspoken,

"Would I be so exasperated if it was?" There's your opening: What does she have to lose by following your advice? Her discipline—or what looks like discipline—is only eroding her authority. She can't honestly want to navigate parenthood like that. It's a direct relationship: the more frustration, the more open one is to guidance.

Next, ask Mom if she'll agree to a time trial. Will she implement your ideas for one month? At the end of the month, even if improvement is by the inch, that's forward progress, evidence of good advice.

Granted, you can't know how well she is practicing your preaching. You're not in her house. A challenge in any kind of counseling, personal or professional, is transferring words into action.

A mother of a four-year-old asked me to spend a few sessions in her home showing her how to get better at discipline. She wanted to see firsthand how I would do what I advised her to do, and if it didn't work, how I would adjust. Would your daughter be agreeable to something similar? It needn't be in her home. It could be anywhere—in your home, at a restaurant, the park, the parole office.

"They don't misbehave for me." Don't repeat that to Mom. She already doubts her discipline competence. Besides, they will misbehave for you, if Mom is around. She's the one they challenge. That will allow you the opportunity to act on what you've been telling Mom, assuming of course she's willing to allow you.

Ask her: "Do you think I raised you well?" If yes, follow with, "Don't you think what I did would be good for your own kids?"

If no or she waffles, accept it, and next time she comes to you for guidance, mostly listen. Apparently, she has some misgivings about your childrearing and wants to go in a different direction, though that direction is leading to frustration.

All of this assumes that you're giving good advice. Most grandparents do. Their instincts are honed by experience and commonsense wisdom accumulated by countless generations before them. As part of this generation, your daughter may be swayed by so-called enlightened notions, many of which sound good on paper but don't work too well with real kids. So while your daughter is trying to do all the right things, she is flummoxed by the wrong outcome. So she turns to you, her prime source for mothering.

Her ongoing frustration should clear her ears. Stand ready to talk.

Elmer Fudd Advice or "I feel caught in the middle."

My daughter phones me upset with her husband. I want to be supportive, but I feel caught in the middle.

In the memorable words of that life guru Elmer Fudd, "Be quiet; be vewwy, vewwy quiet."

A parent is routinely an adult child's go-to for advice about life—childrearing, marriage, finances. When that child voices frustration over a spouse, a parent has to be careful in how she listens and what she supports.

A parallel can be drawn to marriage counseling, which can be likened to walking a tightrope. On one hand, the therapist listens to both spouses, maintaining some neutrality, at least for a time. On the other, the therapist knows he or she is hearing two perspectives, and the challenge is to balance them without upsetting either spouse too much.

To say that spouses can sound as though they inhabit different houses is an understatement. Sometimes they sound as though they inhabit different planets. Is one or both deliberately presenting a false picture to gain the therapist as an ally? Not typically. More often, each is portraying the marriage as he or she sees it.

Unless your son-in-law is weighing in on a conference call, you are hearing one voice: your daughter's. However reasonable, it is still subjective, colored by her personal reading of circumstances. Even if it dovetails with what you know about your son-in-law, you don't have the complete picture. You're not on the inside. Keep in mind a basic law of therapy: Respect the limits of your knowledge.

A client will tell me of her devastation upon discovering her spouse's extramarital relationship. For added support, she has also talked about it with close friends or family. Slowly, she and he are saving their marriage. Others, though, who heard her pain, may still view the unfaithful spouse as a creep who doesn't deserve forgiveness. Her relationship with him is healing, but theirs with him is damaged.

Does your daughter call during high emotion? Could she later calm, reach an accord, or at least a truce, with her husband? They are doing better, but you may not know that. Her distress is still ringing in your ears.

Whatever your daughter's emotions, control your commiserating. Agreement may be short-term supportive, but it could lead to long-term family complications. Here's a guideline: The angrier your daughter becomes, the quieter you remain.

Then, too, you could be repeated, as in "Even my mother thinks you're (fill in the blank)." During a dispute, citing like-minded allies is meant to lend weight to one's side. You don't want to be cited. Again, your future with your son-in-law is involved.

How do you maneuver out of the middle? Get caller ID and let the call go to voicemail. "Hi. I'm not here right now. I'm on a month-long expedition to the top of Mount Everest. I'll return your call after I climb back down."

If your knees couldn't tolerate more than three flights of stairs, and your daughter knows that, and if you do want to take her calls, you have other less lofty options.

One, listen more than you speak. Listening is far safer than voicing opinions. Speaking wrongly is hard to do when you're not speaking. If your silence is heard as dissent, reply with something like, "I'm just listening so I can understand you better." When unsure what to say, use counselor speak.

Two, ask questions to help your daughter find solutions. "Do you know why John does that? Does he tell you? How does he react when you say that? Is there room to compromise on this?" This moves the focus from "This shouldn't be happening" to "What can I help you do about it?"

Three, avoid critiques. "I always thought John was capable of that. I feel bad that you have to put up with so much. He doesn't appreciate all you do." Some, perhaps all of this may be true, but ask yourself: What benefit does saying so bring to your daughter or her marriage?

At some point, you might just have to confess, "I'm sorry, but I don't want to get in the middle of this. I want what's best for you and John and the kids, and my stepping in could only add problems." If you aren't afraid of wading into perilous water, you could add, "I would guess John has his own view of all this."

Heed Elmer's advice when you feel pressed to be empathic and weigh in: "Be vewwy, vewwy quiet."

Silence Is Golden or "I'd better learn to keep my mouth shut."

When I see my grandchildren misbehaving, especially while their parents permit it, it's hard for me to keep quiet, even when I'm not asked my opinion.

There's a piece of tongue-in-cheek wisdom for mothers on a daughter's wedding day: Sit up, shut up, and wear beige. It's also wise counsel for grandparents witnessing misconduct, though dressing neutral might be much easier than holding one's tongue.

Does this mean a comment wouldn't be accurate? No. That it wouldn't be helpful? No. That it wouldn't be tactful? No. It means that if it isn't sought, it might not be well received. It could be ignored or rejected outright.

If you've spoken up before, what was the reaction? Silence? Defensiveness? Excuses? Gratitude? "Why, thank you. I guess I am getting a little sloppy in my discipline. It's good you're here to guide me." Uh-huh.

If you want to gauge how others will respond to your opinion, ask yourself, "How have they responded in the past?" The best predictor of future behavior is past behavior under similar conditions. If they don't want to hear something the first five times it's said, they're not likely to warm to it the next twenty times.

Can you speak more freely with a child than with her spouse?

More often than not, yes. This doesn't mean in-laws are naturally more defensive. It means that the parent-child relationship typically affords more leeway to comment. At that, unless both spouses want to hear you, it's wise to sit up and shut up. Your relationship with either won't suffer, and neither will their relationship with each other because of you. You want what's best for your grandchild. Acting badly is not. That makes it all the more tough to restrain yourself. Still, you are not the parent. For better or worse, her parents are the main disciplinarians.

Should you never say a word about Angelina's conduct? Not necessarily. If she's disrespectful or nasty toward you, you have every right to speak up, however her parents might react. It is one thing for them to allow unruly behavior toward themselves. That is their choice. It is quite another for you to allow it toward you. You are not telling Angelina's mom or dad how to raise her; you are putting legitimate boundaries on how you expect to be treated.

Then too, discipline is not always a matter of a right way or a wrong way. Differences may be ones of style and approach. How the parents discipline may not be how you would or did with your children.

Time can be your ally. If your grandchildren's behavior grows more troublesome with age (a common trajectory), the parents may start to feel it. And grandparents are turned to more often than therapists. "Mom, what would you have done if we acted like this? Dad, any ideas on how to manage him?" Past silence will give you more present credibility.

That's my opinion anyway. You did ask.

Stopping Whining and Tantrums (S.W.A.T.) or
"We spanked but they don't."

We spanked our children when we thought appropriate. Our daughter is absolutely against spanking her three- and five-year-old, who, I'm sorry to say, are getting pretty bratty.

In only a generation or two, spanking has posted a meteoric rise on the list of childrearing sins. Most in our generation saw it as one good discipline option. Many in the present generation see it, at best, as a very last resort or a necessary evil. The experts are overwhelmingly opposed, parents are mixed, and to be expected, almost all kids vote no, as they do most any discipline.

Why the rapid generational turnaround? The main push comes from the professionals. They have smacked it from every angle. Spanking teaches aggression, it solves problems through force, it is big people intimidating little people, it sends mixed messages, and most ominously, it is a form of child abuse.

Quite a list of indictments, theoretically anyway. What does reality and objective research say? What grandparents and endless generations before them knew: When done in a loving home, under emotional control, and offense-specific, spanking commits none of these sins. Bad spanking, if you will, can indeed hurt a child's emotional development. The critical word is *bad*. Spanking alone doesn't cause the trouble, but erratic, heavy-handed overreaction can. What's more, poor spanking routinely is part of overall poor parenting. Put another way, it is not spanking itself that is bad, it is bad spanking along with bad parenting.

Though I have no actual statistics—few saw the need to survey this controversy a few generations ago—my experience is that twice those in your generation saw few drawbacks to a measured swat or two on the bottom than does this generation. Further, judging by actual statistics, children then showed much lower rates of unruliness, aggression, and pathology. If spanking by itself—no matter the type or context—leads to all manner of psychological ills, where was the evidence for that when spanking was a far more common practice?

It's no surprise that your daughter has a never-ever mindset about spanking. Because the experts have few good or even neutral words for the practice, likely your daughter has absorbed their perspective. In her mind, your childrearing was of another time and society, not necessarily translatable to hers.

My book *Back to the Family* presents the findings of a nation-wide survey of strong families. It asks, "How are you raising such admirable children?" Approximately 70 percent of the parents said they had spanked, do spank, or would spank. Thirty percent said they don't and never have. Your daughter right now is in the 30 percent.

Spanking must be judged as all disciplinary practices must. How well does this work, in your home, with your values and your child's personality? Chastity may have been spanked twice in her six years, reacting with a tearful, "I'm really, really, really sorry, Daddy. I'll paint the basement for you." Spike, after receiving a hand-delivered message that clearly should have been felt, stares back, "Is that it? You wrinkled my pajamas."

Even if you could persuade your daughter that her children would benefit from a firmer hand, she's not comfortable nor confident doing so. Consequently, her children's reaction would probably be more resistance, confirming for her, "It doesn't work. It only makes them act worse."

Give up trying to nudge her to do what you did. For whatever reasons, she is not imitating all of your disciplinary ways. The standard argument, "You turned out just fine," may also not persuade her. She may not think she turned out as fine as you do. Or if she did, she may not believe spanking had much to do with it.

"I'm sorry to say, they can be pretty bratty." Most likely it's not any lack of spanking that is leading to the brattiness. It may be that, as your daughter strives to do everything right as a mother, she has become confused by the press of theories and trendy notions. The kids sense this and push harder. It's not the absence of her spanking that is fostering the brattiness; it's the presence of permissiveness.

If the kids' opposition grows as they do, your advice and experience may one day be sought. Wait quietly for that day. Be careful to avoid any tone that says, "I was wondering when you'd see it." By then, the kids may have aged out of being spanked. The need for firm discipline, however, knows no age limits. Talk about how she can be a stronger mom, and that she doesn't need to spank to be one.

On the other hand (sorry), it isn't always younger parents

who are antispanking. Grandma or Grandpa can have a change of mind. Once they were okay with a swat on their own child's bottom, now they cringe or bristle when Dad or Mom does the same to little Fanny. While the adult-child notes the irony: "Hey, what was good for us is bad for our kids?"

Stay your hand. For sure, don't get dramatic. Don't throw your body between parent and child. You may disagree, but that doesn't mean they're wrong. As said here often, the parental prerogative on how to discipline is paramount.

Besides, if you lived every day with Fanny, you'd probably find yourself returning to your former spanking ways.

Grandparent to the Rescue or "Maybe I shouldn't have stepped in."

I think my son is too strict in disciplining his children. Usually I don't say much about it. Recently he put his young daughter in the corner for something I wouldn't. On impulse, I corrected him and released her. He got very upset at me.

"I don't say much about it." You leave your words in your head. You may think them, but you don't say them. Smart.

"Usually." Meaning, you do let them out occasionally. Sometimes you agree; sometimes you don't. But as long as you don't actively interfere, your son may not react. If you do interfere, as you see, he will.

My word for it is *undercutting*. It is the act of deliberately undoing a parent's discipline in front of both parent and child. Undercutting involves more than words. "He didn't mean to push his sister; he was just in a hurry to get past her." Undercutting is action. If put into words, it conveys, "Your dad (mom) is being mean. They don't understand you like I do. I'll fix it."

"But that's not my intent." Even if not, that's how the child can read it. Parent, too.

When a grandparent thinks her son/daughter is too strict, I ask, "Is he a good parent? Is he in any way abusive? Does he discipline differently than you would? Does he discipline differently than you did?" Typically the answers are yes, no, yes, no, which reveals that "too strict" is more a difference of opinion than a reality.

"But I worry about my grandchild's well-being." Is there love in the home? Is he a pretty happy little guy? Is he pleasant to be around? Much of the time, the answers are yes, yes, and yes— further confirmation that the concern is based in emotion, as the grandparent feels bad when Will gets disciplined and thus is moved to protect him.

Why do you think your son got so upset? After all, you didn't move to discipline his daughter when he didn't. On the contrary, you were benevolent, releasing her from her ordeal, giving a hug and kiss in the process, consoling, "It's better now. Daddy didn't mean it. He's sorry." You didn't say that, did you?

Your son got angry not only because you overruled him, but because you made him look unfair in front of his daughter. Further, you stepped in as her defender, raising the chances she'll be more unruly whenever her defender is nearby.

The littlest of kids learn quickly to scan their surroundings for anyone who can rescue them from a parent's discipline. Only a few rescues can construct a discipline meme:

Mommy/Daddy mean; Grandpa/Grandma nice.

One of our children sought my permission to do something for which his mother had already said no. (Appealing the decision is a mainstay childhood strategy.) I said, "If it were up to me, I'd let you." Dumb! Dumb! Dumb! When my wife found out—the child told her 6.4 seconds later—she reacted strongly. Why? As she rightfully maintained, I had hung her discipline out to dry. I became the flexible parent; she the inflexible one. Not only was this wrong, but it was unfair to my wife. It took me about eight more I-agree-with-Moms to quash further appeal tactics.

"I don't say much about his discipline usually." Drop the "usually," and for sure don't wade in unless invited, preferably in writing, preferably notarized.

One, Two, Three, Too Many? or "How can they handle that many kids?"

My daughter and son-in-law have three children, ages five, three, and one. She is pregnant with her fourth. I think her plate is already full, and I worry about her stress level.

Does she think her plate is full? Is she feeling stressed? Is more motherhood what she wants?

Have you said anything to your daughter about your misgivings? If you have, I suggest you say no more. If you haven't, don't.

A father told me that after their third child, neither he nor his wife announced, "We're pregnant." From most friends and family, the reactions were less than enthusiastic. With each pregnancy, however, the commentary dwindled. Probably it had something to do with their being tagged a lost cause, people who wanted more kids no matter what anyone thought.

More grandparents are expressing concerns like yours. Ironically, they themselves had four, five, six kids, or more, raising them with far fewer conveniences—material and otherwise—than today's parents. In smaller houses, too.

Why this shift in attitude? Some of it reflects the reigning cultural view of the ideal family: one boy, one girl. Three children are acceptable if the first two are the same sex. "You're trying to get your boy/girl, right?" What if the first three are the same sex? Well, time to accept genetics.

My wife and I met something similar as we adopted more children. Long about child number six, we began to hear, "Are you done? Why so many?" My standard answer was, "Tax deductions. We'll stop when I pay zero taxes."

My all-time favorite comeback was from a mother of seven. Trooping through somewhere with all seven in tow, if asked, "Are these all your kids?" she'd reply, "Oh no, the oldest is at home with the triplets." That stopped most people in mid-comment, until one day the four-year-old asked, "Really, can I see them?"

Most likely, your daughter is hearing similar critiques, increasingly as her fourth pregnancy becomes obvious. In a society where 40-plus percent of babies are born to single mothers, why is it that women having babies within marriage are facing such social judgment?

I suspect your daughter didn't anticipate this. I also suspect she's getting pretty sensitive about it. Others may not understand her, but if her mother does, that's what matters most.

Observe your daughter's demeanor. For the most part, is it upbeat, even when frazzled? Then be reassured. Resist future projecting: "Well, things may be going OK now, but it'll get more complicated as they get older." After all, someday they'll be teenagers, drivers, college loan applicants. Yes, the demands do shift with age. Demands don't necessarily mean stress. At one point, nine family cars sat in our driveway. The insurance wasn't that bad. It only totaled $110…a day. Bigger families find ways to make it work. They have to.

Mothers of several are often reluctant to talk of their normal, everyday frustrations. They know they could face reactions like,

"Well, what did you expect with that many?" Sometimes the comments show concern mixed with doubt: "Can you give them enough individual attention? Can you juggle it all? Do you have enough bedrooms?" Our house had four bedrooms. We thought it was plenty.

Ask questions that reflect support: "Can I help you arrange the bedrooms? Do you need me to take the younger kids some afternoons so you can run errands? Have you looked into any of Dr. Ray's books?"

The kids themselves calm worries about a family that's too big. Parents who want a bunch of kids highly value family life. As such, they are committed to being good parents, and their kids generally reflect that. With each child, there is more fun, not less; more joy, not less; more love, not less.

As one mother put it, "Love multiplies; it doesn't divide."

Parenthood Replay or "If I could go back, I'd change..."

I have many regrets over how I raised my children. My son is now married with two children, and I see some of my mistakes repeating themselves in his parenting. I can't say much to him because our relationship is fragile.

At your son's birth, did you think, "Let me see how poorly I can raise this child?" Or "I'm going to stand by and watch him raise himself." How about, "Any regrets I'll have are years away, so I won't worry about that now."

No doubt, looking back you'd do things differently. From this distance perhaps you see your younger self as immature, or irresponsible, or self-absorbed. As the adage goes, "We grow too soon old and too late smart."

Looking over one's shoulder, it's easy to have twenty-twenty vision. Few of us have twenty-twenty when looking ahead. Do I mean to downplay your childrearing shortcomings? No. Am I giving you excuses for them? No. Am I saying that you're not alone in looking back with some regret? Yes. Most parents, me included, would make changes if given a second go-around.

"My parenting was worse than most." Maybe, maybe not. How many families' inner workings do you know? I have clients who see themselves as you do. They feel inferior to other parents. Often they aren't. Their comparisons are based upon full knowledge of every squeak and squabble in their own home while being only partially aware, ignorant even, of what's happening in others. Take it from a shrink: what you see isn't always what is. Your childrearing may have been full of faults in your eyes, but not so far out of the norm as you think.

Regrets partner with guilt. As a grandparent, it's time to lay aside your parenting guilt. For two reasons. One, the past. Your younger parenthood is years, perhaps decades, gone. You are sorry for it. That means God forgives you for it. It's time for you to forgive yourself, also.

Two, the present. Guilt interferes with being a good grandparent. It tempts toward overcompensation. Many grandparents admit to overdoing things—materially, financially, permissively—because they feel they underdid things as parents. They shower gifts and goodies too freely. Their discipline becomes lax to make up for overdisciplining as parents. They too quickly correct a grown son or daughter whose mistakes recall for them their own mistakes.

However well-intentioned, none of this rectifies the past. It only complicates the present, causing friction with a grown child who may not want or appreciate the overdoing.

Resist the urge to correct your son when you see him repeating some of your former errors. (You said your relationship is already fragile.) Focus on correcting yourself. Be a better grandparent than you were a parent. Be present—at games, activities, school events. Spend more time than money on the kids. Listen better to children and parents. In short, do what you would do if you could revisit your young parenthood.

You've got grandchildren. You've been given a do-over. Leave the regrets in the past. Take advantage of the present.

Religion Resistance or "My kids don't want the religion they were raised with."

My daughter is not raising her children in the religious beliefs that she was raised in. When I try to introduce to my grandchildren a few practices—grace before meals, prayers, picture bibles—she gets upset and tells me not to push my religion upon her children.

Adult children who leave the faith of their youth are an ongoing source of sadness, often self-blame, for their parents. Whatever your second-guessing over how you raised your daughter, it is now intensified by how she is raising her children.

Do you feel somehow responsible for this generational turn of affairs? If only you'd been more (fill in the blank). If only you'd been less (fill in the blank). The greater your guilt over past mistakes, the stronger your drive to correct the present.

Your intentions are sincere, but you face a major hurdle: Your daughter, and I'm assuming her husband, doesn't agree. Her resistance may not be so much rooted in your religion as in her motherhood, specifically its implied deficiencies. She may read your gestures as your way of filling her family's religious gaps.

You are Grandma. But you are not Mom. However misguided you believe she is, she has the right to be misguided. By trying to guide her, not only could you antagonize her, but you could push her and her husband further from any religious attraction. Softening their attitude will be difficult if they feel you are ignoring their wishes. What's more, if your daughter sees no way to restrain you, she could limit your contact with the kids. That is the last thing you want to risk, I'm sure.

My advice: Cease introducing religious practices to your grandkids. Apologize to your daughter and son-in-law for your actions. Assure them you will no longer do anything they would find objectionable. And if there's any question, you will run it by them first. Your foremost goal is a solid, trustworthy relationship.

What if you are the only person in the kids' lives to give them any kind of religious exposure? Even so, you can't impose something that isn't wanted. But what if the kids want it? Again, their parents don't, and they are the ones deciding for them, for the present anyway. If, however, Mom sees the kids being interested, she may rethink her own stance. A history of faith-filled childhood memories is likely still lingering somewhere in her.

Within your daughter's limits, you are still able to teach your grandchildren about God. How? By being the best grandma you can be to the whole family. By being caring, cooperative and easy to get along with. All will see that Grandma is a really neat lady, and her religion is a big part of that. The combination is winsome.

Through it all, don't get discouraged. Many adults take a second look at the faith of their childhood as their own children age. They come to realize and value what they were given as children.

Their children lead them back home.

Change of Life Conversion or "I wished I'd believed sooner."

I returned to church after my two children were married with children. I've got lots of guilt over all those lost years. Now they are raising their children with no religion, as I raised them.

Be grateful that God opened your eyes. While he has transformed your life later than you'd like, a late conversion is infinitely better than no conversion.

Of course, had you stayed where you once were, you wouldn't be nagged by guilt. Nevertheless, awareness is almost always preferable to ignorance. It is better to feel bad over what was missed than to never know what was missed. The saying is: We grow too soon old and too late smart.

Conversion brings forgiveness. God pardons what you did or didn't do as a mother. You loved your children as you knew how, as you thought best, though you now know your thinking could have been more complete.

Your family may be confused by you. Who is this person anyway? Where was all this when we were growing up? They may even want their old mom back. Are they thinking, "Well, that's good for Mom, but it's not where we're at. Nor our children."

Adult conversions can still reverberate through a generation or two. To strengthen the reverberation, don't push or preach. Understandably, your first impulse is to impart now what you didn't then. Indeed, you might feel a moral obligation to do so. Read the cues. If your children invite input, engage. If not, ease up. Your children are not where you are, and you can't press them to be. It took you decades to get there.

Show similar discretion with your grandchildren. While they may be more interested, especially the younger ones, your latitude to speak on matters of faith is still set by their parents. You are courting trouble by seeking opportunities not approved by Mom or Dad. Much as you might wish to share your enthusiasm, you have to respect the parents' limits. The last thing you want is for your conversion to be a source of family friction.

Entertain any and all whys. Be ready to explain what you believe and how you came to believe it. Let the openings be supplied by others. Depending upon how wide the openings are, ask your own questions. Ask your family what they think of the new you. How do they see you, for better or worse? Your intent is not to defend, argue, or sound superior. You are seeking to understand, not necessarily to alter.

The suggestion from a few paragraphs ago is relevant again: Show all, young and older, that Grandma is a very easy person to like. She's kinder, more thoughtful, and a better listener. Whatever it is that Grandma believes, one thing is sure: She is more loving and giving with her family. In the end, that will win them over more than words.

A closing question: Can I assume every member of your family is younger than you, the grandkids a whole lot younger? They're where you once were, with a key difference: They have a good model to watch and learn from.

It's Grandma's Fault or "Why am I getting blamed for this?"

My son and his wife do not take their three children to church.
He says it is because we forced him to go as a teenager, and he
refuses to force his children.

Of all the reasons given for abandoning religion, your son's is in the top ten. Of all the true reasons, it's nowhere near the top ten. Often cited, believed even, it's a faux reason. Children move away from their religious upbringing for many intertwined reasons: secular pressures, immoral conduct, apathy, self-pursuits. A common theme in therapy: People are often unaware or mistaken about the actual motives behind their conduct. "I was forced to go to church" is a facile rationale that, while covering other motives, also arouses second-guessing and guilt in one's parents.

Blaming parents for poor adult choices has gained a good bit of psychological traction in recent generations. The childrearing professionals have broadcast relentlessly about the untoward and long-range repercussions of psychologically poor parenting. No wonder so many adult children believe "it's not my bad moves now; it's my parent's bad moves then."

Few would dispute that bad parenting can lead to all manner of child and adulthood trouble. The twist these days is that good, loving, however imperfect, moms and dads are getting the blame for their grown children's decisions. Your son's refusal to expose his children to religion is his decision. Identifying you as the culprit is not only unfair but raises the questions: Why is he holding you responsible? What motives is he ignoring or denying?

Grandparents swallow a double dose of guilt. It's bad enough that their child has drifted from the faith, but he is taking his children with him. Two generations are affected.

What if you could have done better back then? Even so, to be fair to yourself, you must consider the whole picture. Your parenting is a factor in your son's personality. It is not the only one. His temperament, free choices, the cultural forming of his attitudes—all interact to shape how he thinks today. Put another way, rarely can a parent take sole blame for his adult child's actions.

Resist pushing your son toward church. First, since he holds you accountable for opposing his adolescent will, he's not likely to submit his adult will.

Second, he won't like hearing that he is religiously short-changing his children. He believes he is being balanced and flexible. He is determined not to do what he believes, however erroneously, you did to him.

Third, though you might want to correct your past parenting mistake, there's nothing to correct. You have nothing to apologize for. You did what you believed best. Pressing your son now will likely stiffen his resistance.

Suppose you could go back and remove your church requirement. Would you do it? Would you free your son, allowing his youthful shortsightedness to decide for or against church? Not very likely. Your aim was to expose him to faith, not pressure him. How he ultimately reacted was not your doing.

You may not be able to influence your son's church stance and how that impacts his children. You can refuse, however, to take the blame for it.

You can also hope and pray for a softening that will move him back to his preteen faith.

To Love, Not Condone or "I don't want them to think I approve of that."

My granddaughter is twenty-one and lives with her boyfriend. We and her parents morally have a problem with this. It's been over a year, and I'm still uneasy around her.

How uneasy are you, and how much does she sense it? Are your times together tense, consequently leading to fewer of them? The natural course of an uneasy relationship is toward less contact.

No doubt, you wish to stay close to your granddaughter, even as she continues to stay close to her boyfriend. Yet, you don't wish to condone their housekeeping. How do you mesh the two? They aren't as incompatible as they seem. Staying close to someone does not mean you have to celebrate or even agree with their choices.

Above all, love her. You have a history together. Draw upon it. This might not come so naturally with the boyfriend, as he's relatively new to your life. Still, treat both with respect and dignity. Doing so does not mean you are fine with their living arrangements.

Loving your granddaughter means you haven't changed toward her. You are not emotionally cooler, more distant, or less approachable. Your intent is not to punish her until she straightens up. It is to treat her the same as you did before she lived with the boyfriend.

Whether her relationship with him weakens or strengthens, you want to keep your relationship with her stable. It's your best way to influence her, if not now, someday.

Resist reiterating your moral stance. Should your granddaughter broach the matter, the door is open to talk. If you reopen it, you'll probably accomplish little other than to invite more strain between you. Conversations can get stiff when one or both parties anticipate a touchy subject lurking around the next sentence.

Understandably, your uneasiness can follow the flow of the conversation. "Grandma, you should see the couch we bought. It's a lot like the one you have. We are looking for a different apartment, something nicer than the one we're in. When are you coming over to have dinner and see our place?"

How do you react when she talks and acts as a wife with a husband? Conversationally. Ask about the couch, the apartment. Talk as you would with anyone else. You're not emotionally gushing, as in, "That is just so wonderful. I am so happy for you." Rather, you are showing a pleasant interest.

"I'm not sure about dinner." Certainly that is your prerogative. Again, though, if you do accept the invitation, you are not accepting the implication of the invitation. You are keeping a connection with your granddaughter.

"What if my granddaughter reads my reaction as acceptance of her lifestyle?" How long has your granddaughter known you? Does she have a pretty good idea of your beliefs and why? How likely is she to think, "This is great. My grandmother is coming around. It took her all these decades, but she's finally agreeing with me."

Most likely, your granddaughter does hope your moral vision will blur. She wants your approval. Even so, you needn't reemphasize your moral position every time you think she thinks your warmth means blanket approval. (No pun intended.) For years, you have been clear both in words and by your life. You can't control how she interprets you now.

Your love for your granddaughter and her boyfriend is your best means to morally move them. Without a good relationship, you won't have much of a chance to persuade her. When her conduct causes the most discomfort for you, you might have to look like you're comfortable around her. In the end, it will be worth it, for both of you.

Whether one day she and her boyfriend break up, marry, or have separate domiciles, your bridge with her will have remained solid. There will be no lingering resentments toward you. "Well, Grandma, now you like me because I'm good again."

Your warmth doesn't give her your permission to do the live-in thing. It conveys that your love is not conditional. And that's what will last, even if her relationship with her boyfriend doesn't.

Holiday Competition or "I wish we had more of their time during the holidays."

Thanksgiving, Christmas and Easter are holidays of negotiation between us, my daughter's family, and her in-laws. I realize the need to divide time, but I feel like we get the leftovers.

It's the holiday hop. Who goes where, when, and for how long before switching houses? Split or blended families add even more steps to the dance.

Grandparents are sensitive to the distribution of time. For them, holidays are full of history, years of family gatherings in one home—theirs. The shifting sharing of holidays for the most part is accepted, but not without some nostalgia for the old days.

Ideally, the itinerary unfolds without too many glitches and with goodwill toward all. Realistically, however, imbalances occur, with one side getting less than a fair share of time. The reasons vary: distance, family size, undue pressure, schedules, single parents, divorce custody arrangements.

Grandparents feel most shorted when they interpret the holiday portions as indicating preference; that is, my child and his/her spouse seem to favor the other side over us. It doesn't soothe doubts if the explanations sound weak. "We meant to stop by earlier, but the kids were tired. By the time we noticed, most of the day had slipped away. We'll come over this weekend. The kids can open their gifts then."

Your daughter may be feeling the reason is pressure from the other side. Trying to keep peace, she yields, knowing that you will be more gracious about it. In a way, that's a compliment. She knows you are the more accommodating grandparent, unwilling to put her in a lose-lose position.

Then, too, her spouse may be the one applying the pressure. He is pushing hard for his parents, out of loyalty, obligation, guilt, or feeling their pressure. Somebody has to be the more flexible spouse, and your daughter has decided, all things considered, to be the one.

It's always good to look at oneself. Is your holiday house relaxed and pleasant, or sprinkled with tension? Bickering? Complaining? Sour moods? From you or Great-uncle Fred? Ask your daughter how she sees the holiday atmosphere at your place. You'll get a glimpse of what needs to be done to make it nicer for all.

Whatever the reasons for the holiday disparity, control what you can: Be agreeable. Don't pressure from your direction. Don't pull out the time sheets from the last four holidays to make your case. For sure, don't use guilt. What you gain in winning time by guilt, you lose in winning willingness. You want your daughter's family to freely choose to visit.

"If I don't speak up, nothing will change." Speaking up could influence them to adjust their schedule, but what would be their motive? To appease? What's more, if the in-laws are applying heat, would you be setting up a dueling grandparents scenario? It benefits you to rise above a holiday tug of war. In the long run, you're more likely to see more of your family.

"Won't we be accepting whatever time we get?" Does your daughter know how much you value family? Did she grow up knowing that? If so, she'll probably see you moved more by kindness than indifference. She may well know you'd like more holiday time, but she also well knows you're not about to force it.

Competition for holiday attention across grandparents can create both friction and distance. Don't compete. It's the best way to win.

Inequity Is Fair or "They say we overdo at Christmas."

My son has asked us for the past couple of Christmases to limit our gifts for the grandkids. The other grandparents have not, so I don't feel we should have to. And what would the kids think?

Once upon a Christmas, after all the gift exchanging, unwrapping, and oohs and aahs, my mother handed me one last box. In it was a check for some odd dollars and cents.

"Mom, what's this?"

She replied, "I spent a little more on the other kids, and I wanted to even it out."

Overwhelmed by Christmas good cheer, I said, "Even it out? I thought I was your favorite. I am the oldest." Okay, I didn't. My wife would have made me give back the check.

Mom's box reflected her bias to be exquisitely fair. I did notice, however, that as we added more kids, she measured the gift totals a little more loosely. My sisters each had three kids; we had ten. By the numbers, then, we should have gotten 233 percent more. The law of supply and demand eventually ruled, I guess.

The moral of the story? Grandparents have a bent to be equitable whenever and however possible, not wanting in the slightest to appear to have favorites. (A few do play favorites, a topic for later.) Christmas, more so than birthdays, can bring out the equity impulse.

For one, typically more family is present. Everyone can see what everyone got and gave. No one wants to appear Scroogey. Two, kids aren't good at faking their reactions. Socks and pajamas fall at the bottom of the enthusiasm hierarchy. Video games and technology sit at the top. The older kids lean toward cash. A grandparent wants to see excitement, if not always for quality, then quantity.

Three, Christmas evokes the spirit of material generosity. Gifts can say, "See how much I love you."

All this can move grandparents to gift freely, while moving parents to slow down the flow of gifts.

What is your course? Cooperate. Agree or not, accept your son's wishes. You may see no problem with your total, but he sets the limits. Resist, too, the temptation to hold some gifts for the future. I think your son will get suspicious if a Christmas sweater shows up on February 23.

"The other grandparents are not cutting back." You can't do much about that. They and the parents are in separate negotiations. They may be resisting to the point of conflict. Your aim is to avoid conflict.

"What if my son and his wife have made their request only of us?" Perhaps the other grandparents already self-limit the gifts. Or, perhaps there is a double standard at play. Again, though this scenario seems unfair, accept it graciously. Forgo any attitude that says, "Why do we have to if they don't. That doesn't seem right." Nonetheless, you're smarter to be amenable. If nothing else, your son will appreciate that you're not provoking a Christmas controversy that keeps on giving.

"Couldn't my grandkids think I love them less?" Than whom? Grandpa Rich and Grandma Penny? That would seem to depend upon the nature of your relationship. If it's good all year through, the kids won't rethink it at Christmas. They may not even care about gift disparities. Unless you dole out socks and pajamas. That could test your bond.

By honoring your son's request, you have little to lose and much to gain. You'll sow Christmas goodwill. The effect on the grandkids should be minimal, materially and emotionally. And you'll reduce your Christmas expenses. Give the savings to a charity in the kids' names.

As my family grew in size, my mom's gift cost per child dropped. And I got a bigger compensation check.

The Spoiler or "What's wrong with a little spoiling?"

My daughter says I overdo it with the gifts and goodies for my grandchildren, ages nine, seven, and two. I think a grandmother should be able to spoil her grandkids.

It's a stereotype, but it's wrapped around some truth. Grandparents do have a little more Disney in them than parents. The questions follow: How much Disney is too much? And who decides?

Some grandparents pull up in the Toys "R" Us semi, announcing, "I'll be back. These eighteen-wheelers aren't big enough to haul everything in just one trip anymore." Others keep the goodie spigot slow but steady.

Grandma: Look at this cute little stuffed zebra I found at a yard sale.

Parent: Mom, it's nice, but she already has thirty-four stuffed animals.

Grandma: I know, but she doesn't have a zebra.

Parent: She has seven horsey stuffed animals.

Grandma: But this one is so cute and tiny. She can carry it with her in the car.

Parent: Mom, have you seen the car? There are six stuffed animals sitting in there.

Grandma: Yes, but I noticed they're all in the back seat. There are none in the front seat.

OK, this an exaggeration, sort of, at least the part about the back seat. There are only three back there.

What is the difference between doing and overdoing? Let's first define *spoiling*. Are we talking time, affection, playfulness? In other words, spoiling in the intangibles? These are seldom a point of contention between generations. Most parents are grateful when grandparents are gracious with the gifts of a good relationship. Friction only results if Mom or Dad feel they are in competition with a grandparent for a child's affection. That's another topic.

Far more often, spoiling means in the stuff sense. Your daughter probably doesn't mind your material largesse, up to a point. Her argument lies in the gap between your largesse and her limits.

"I can't see any harm in getting them a few things here and there." If it were "a few things here and there," would your daughter see any harm either? Most parents accept a grandparent's doling out more goodies than they do. If they're working hard to meet the basics, some extras from a grandparent are welcome. It's when the extras flow from a seemingly endless reservoir that parents worry about their effects upon the kids.

"I don't think I overdo it." Suppose we polled a hundred grandparents and suppose seventy-three agree with you. Poll one hundred parents, and fifty-six of them agree with you. By the numbers, you have strong intergenerational support. What does it mean? Nothing. Only one vote counts: your daughter's. Even if the majority poll her unreasonable, her reasoning out-polls them. She has veto power.

"I don't want the kids to think I'm cheap with them, or don't care about them as much as I do the other grandchildren." OK then, blame Mom. Just kidding, bad advice.

First of all, you're not being cheap with them. You're still generous, just not to the degree that you'd like. More important, I'm sure you're not skimping on the real stuff, like love, time, games. Can you still play flag football? How about Monopoly? Your presence is far more valuable than your presents. And the kids feel it. In ways that really matter, you are not shortchanging them.

"Can't I try to persuade my daughter?" Sure, show her the poll results. Even then, a parent's decisions are not formed by consensus. Mom and Dad alone set the ceiling on gifts, even if ninety-nine other parents would set a higher ceiling. Didn't you afford yourself the same decision-making power when you were raising your daughter? Didn't you ever say, "If all the other kids jump in the lake, are you going to jump in, too?" You should have. It's a classic.

Actually, your daughter is doing you a favor. She's saving you money. Right now, Harley is happy with a toy motorcycle. In a few years, it could take more, like a snowmobile or a big-screen TV.

Too Much Pride or "Stop me before I brag some more."

I've gotten into a habit of bragging too much about my grandchildren. I have friends who do the same about their grandkids. It's a stereotype, but it's rooted in reality. Grandparents can get on a real roll promoting their grandchildren to just about anyone willing to listen and even to those who aren't. It's an understandable urge born of familial pride and pleasure. Put two or more grandparents together with similar urges, however, and a brag battle can begin.

Grandparent #1: My grandson was potty trained in just three days, a week before he turned two.

Grandparent #2: My granddaughter told her parents that she was ready to use the potty just after she blew out the candles at her first birthday. She'd been speaking in complete sentences since she was six months old.

Grandparent #3: All of my daughter's children were pretty much trained about three months out of the womb. The oldest, who was only three, trained the baby.

The annual Christmas family letter puts pride on paper.

My granddaughter, Emmy, is now eleven and just completed her tenth consecutive year of ballet, gymnastics, competitive power lifting, and Greco-Roman language scholarship. She's gearing up for her Olympic try-outs in 2020. Hopefully they won't interfere with her selection as junior ambassador to NATO.

Her brother, Sterling, was surprised on his sixth birthday with calls from the pope, the president, and the ghost of Elvis. He couldn't talk long, though, because we all had to leave for a six-day cruise honoring him for winning our state's 2017 First-Grader of the Year Award.

The real achiever of the family, though, is big brother, Forbes, who last month...

Be honest. How far do you actually read a letter of that stripe? In my feistier days, I was tempted to grade them for grammar and content and return them. Fortunately, I have a wife with better judgment.

Pictures. In the old days, cameras made pictures, which had to be developed (not always—Instamatic cameras anyone?) and primarily were shown to those in one's nearby social circle. Now the sky is the limit—literally. Video texts, Facebook, Instagram, email attachments—all can declare to the world, "Here's my grandchild. Is she cute or what?"

This is not to impugn these modes of contact. They do make possible a level of heretofore unavailable, expansive sharing of one's delight in family life. They are a loving grandparent talking, I mean sending. The risk again lies in overdoing it. What is so meaningful to us may not reach the same level for others. How many folks outside your closest social sphere are all that excited to know that Babe got two hits in his Little League game? One in which they didn't keep score or give a winner's trophy? You could video text his participation trophy.

So how do you talk—text or video—in a more measured way? You've already started: your wish to stop. When you hear yourself boasting, cut yourself off (midsentence?). With practice, you'll get better at stopping sooner, eventually to the point of not starting. Part of being a gracious conversationalist is hearing when you're not being one.

A second strategy: Show more interest in the talker—her kids, grandkids, and life. Redirect the flow of the interchange back to him or her. Ask questions. Seek details. Rather than waiting for your turn to talk, give her extra time. Even if she dominates, your main aim is to slow your pace of promotion. You are effectively pulling out of any my-grandchild-your-grandchild volley.

A perceptive conversationalist will sense what you are doing. She might even be moved to ask about your grandchildren. "Oh my, I've been going on and on. Tell me about your grandson." Now, at least you've got permission to brag a bit.

If you do boast, stick with the facts. Don't embellish. "Well, we think little Newton has a great future as a nuclear particle physicist. At least that's what his preschool teacher says."

Doing or Overdoing? or "Am I spoiling too much?"

I enjoy giving to my grandchildren. But I wonder: When does generosity become spoiling?

How much is too much is guided by much: how many grandkids, their ages, their attitude, their gratitude, your wallet, the parents' wallet, the parents' limits, your spouse's limits.

Numbers alone can put a ceiling on largesse. With additional grandkids, assuming your resources aren't unlimited, your pie is split into ever-smaller pieces. With our first two children, my parents' pie was divided in two. By the time Liz arrived, our number ten, the pie had been cut so many times that her share was a sliver. She did get the leftovers, though, most of them broken or worn out.

Here are a few rules to moderate your material impulses.

Rule #1. Don't give all you are able to or want to. You may be at a life stage where your expenses have decreased and your disposable income has increased. Thus the temptation: I can afford to, so why not? Indeed, many grandparents relish being able to give to their grandchildren in ways they couldn't with their own children.

As a child, when asking my father for a twenty-five-cent raise in my allowance, I had to fill out a six-page financial disclosure form, submit a budget, and listen to a lecture on fiscal frugality.

When Dad would visit our family, he'd walk in announcing, "Any children here need some grandpa dollars?" His new fiscal policy had nothing to do with inflation.

Ability and desire have to be moderated. Otherwise, they will drive spoiling.

A child's reaction can move a grandparent to overdo it: a hug; a "Love you, Thank you so much, You're the best grandma of all"; or a "Mom and Dad would never get me this." While this is nice to hear and can be motivating, it's not necessarily a good guide for giving. A youngster's momentary pleasure is not a sign of what's good for him long term. Kids are not the most mature judges of how much is too much.

Rule #2. Obey a parent's rules. If she thinks you are spoiling, assume you are. "But I don't think I am, and most people would agree with me." Even so, the hand on the spigot is hers. If she wants it turned down, turn it down. Respect a parent's limits. (A recurrent theme in this book.) Parents are the ones who decide what amount of stuff helps or hurts Rich's character.

Rule #3. Observe the kids' attitude. A grandmother told me that one Christmas, her grandkids gave her a catalog with all their gift preferences circled. She viewed it as confirmation that it was time to dial things back. Some grandparents are handed wish lists, sometimes from the kids, sometimes from the parents. Look for signs that an attitude went from gratitude to entitlement.

How do the grandchildren receive the gift? Not all receptions are positive. "I already have one of these. The newer video is a lot better than this one. What can I do with this?" Or the loud absence of any "thank you."

The sentiment is that unless a gift meets my expectations, it will be rebuffed. It's not the latest, the fastest, or the coolest. Sure signs that the level of too much has been reached.

Rule #4. Assess a child's spoil quotient. Some kids are just easier to spoil. Buck checks for goodies behind your back with every visit. Penny seldom thinks to check behind your back. She's too excited to see your face. Either way, reduce the stuff for both. Since Penny isn't that pulled by it, she probably won't even notice any cutback. Buck will, but the reduction will be good for him.

A simple rule: When in doubt about giving too much, give less.

Good Spoiling or "I can't spoil my grandkids. They already are."

My grandchildren, ages eight, six, and three, are very indulged. I was looking forward to doing a little grandparent spoiling, but I don't want to add to their spoiled upbringing.

Grandparent Manual, section 5, paragraph 3C states: "Grandparents, having a beneficial role in a child's life, are granted in certain circumstances a softness and indulgence in their relationship with said grandchild. Exceptions to this permit include but are not limited to:

1) overriding a parent's discipline,
2) sneaking privileges under a parent's radar,
3) purchasing exorbitant and inappropriate gifts,
4) favoring one grandchild over another, and
5) indulging an already indulged child."

Your quandary would seem to fall under exemption 5. The parents have already usurped your grandparent prerogative. They are spoiling beyond what you would ever do, leaving you little flexibility to implement acceptable grandparent status as detailed in section 5, paragraph 3C of the official manual.

Indulged and spoiled are synonymous terms for most people. What exactly do they mean? In the main, they refer to (1) a permissive discipline style and (2) excessive materialism and entertainment. We've addressed the permissive parent style other places in this grandparenting manual. Let's focus here on grandchildren who have been spoiled by materialism.

As long as Mom and Dad are overdoing it, are you handcuffed or reluctant to make a bad situation worse? Until the parents realize that they are guilty of overdoing it, you will probably have to underdo it, that is, to give less material goodies than you'd like. This doesn't prevent you from spoiling your grandkids in other, better ways.

Rather than stuff, choose time and togetherness. Offer slow-paced fun instead of hyperactivated, entertainment-driven options. Choose activities primarily for their shared companionship: listening to Edgar Allen read, taking Bambi to the zoo, accompanying Dusty to the pool, watching a movie with Oscar, building Lego's with Mason, coloring with Art, playing a board game with Wynn. (Sorry, I got on a roll.)

I'll confess, as a young dad, I dozed off about the third page of a child's reading to me. And I lost interest playing trucks on the floor long before they did. As a grandfather, the reverse has occurred. I've got more stamina for doing kid stuff. I can stay conscious for about six pages now.

Some of your activities may seem boring to the kids compared to what they've grown accustomed to, though the two younger ones should more readily cooperate with your idea of spoiling. The oldest may take a little longer. Not much less than the jumbo, megasized, triple chocolate fudge sundae will excite him. Still, you can show all the kids a better side to big-person-little-person fun.

***Spoil* is a negative word.** Can a grandparent spoil positively? Of course. Can she give too much love? Too much time together?

Too much fun? One might argue that even these—excepting love—can be taken to extreme. Still, it's much harder to do so.

When all is done and overdone, you can still do lots of spoiling. It all depends upon how you practice the word.

Grandma Guidance or "I listen, so my grandkids come to me."

My fourteen-year-old granddaughter opens up to me about her troubles with her peers and parents. When she asks my grandma opinion, I'm not always sure what my limits are.

Were it not for grandparents soothing and solving a child's troubles, I suspect counselors would have more business.

Grandparents have experience. They have life wisdom. Perhaps above all, they aren't Mom or Dad. Most grandparents don't have to do the everyday disciplining of a parent. They don't have nearly the disciplinary friction with a child, especially a teen. Thus, they may be seen as safer, more understanding. Interesting, isn't it? As we get older, the kids think we think more like them.

Grandparent guidance parallels professional guidance along several lines. First, you're getting a perspective. Everyone— youngest to oldest—sees people and events through his or her own personal lens. It is extremely difficult, more so for youth, to be 100 percent objective. Therefore, what you are hearing may not be a totally accurate account. Not to say that your granddaughter is deliberately trying to gain your sympathy or allegiance. She just may not be aware how she's coloring things. An experienced counselor recognizes that what she is being told could be slanted, distorted even, by the reality that a human being is doing the telling. No matter how your granddaughter sees it, Dad may, in fact, not be Attila the Hun, and Mom may not be the Wicked Witch of the East.

Second, know that your words—quoted, paraphrased, or altered—could be repeated, not so much to her peers, with whom you carry little weight, but to Mom or Dad. After all, they need to know that it isn't only their daughter who thinks they're wrong. "Even Grandma thinks you're being too strict about this," or "Grandma doesn't understand why you have to be so..." In so many words, "Your own mother agrees with me, not you." Be aware that during your granddaughter's next tiff with a parent, you could be dragged in as a character witness.

The imperative word is *caution*. Listen quickly, speak slowly. It's much harder to misquote silence. Be very slow to agree with your granddaughter when she is unhappy with someone else (read "parent.") "I know, your father can be stubborn. He was like this when he was a little boy."

Because your granddaughter may be hurting, it's natural to sympathize. Yet if sympathy is expressed as, "I agree. Your mom and dad can be really frustrating," you could be asking for a disagreeable encounter should these frustrating people hear about your opinion. It's no shock to them that their daughter thinks they are social Neanderthals. It could shock them that you think so, too. What's more, they may get real upset at you for questioning or undercutting their authority.

What if you do know that your granddaughter's account rings true? You've seen her parents be as she says. Still, avoid recriminations; focus on solutions. She may want from you a friendly ear rather than answers. Nonetheless, help her to solve the problem, if possible, or, if not, to figure out how to live with it.

Third, counselors follow strict rules about confidentiality. What is said in counseling is to stay in counseling. Only in limited circumstances is a therapist required to break confidentiality. These mostly involve the safety and serious welfare of the client or another person.

"Grandma, you have to promise not to tell anyone what I'm going to tell you." That's a promise you'd best not make. "I smoke pot on the weekends with my friends." "My boyfriend wants me to have sex with him." "I met a guy on the internet who wants to get together." Promise you will help however you can, but don't promise to keep a secret if doing so will hurt her.

"If she doesn't get a promise, couldn't she just clam up? Wouldn't that be bad?" The alternative is worse. Agree to full confidence, and there are risks for both of you. If the truth does come to light, as it often does, what happens when Mom and Dad find out what you knew all along? Reassure your granddaughter that, together, you will decide how best to tell her parents. Walk her through the possible results of breaking her silence, stressing that secretiveness brings more complications. Her youth doesn't understand that yet.

What about peer troubles? "My friend is talking suicide." "He is using some serious drugs." "Her cousin sexually molested her." Such matters are much too heavy for a teen to lift by herself. It's good she came to you. Again, reassure her that you will stay by her side at every step as the necessary adults are informed. Initially, she could resist, "She told me this in total confidence. I promised I wouldn't say anything to anybody. She will really be mad at me." Acknowledge that while all of this may be true, a higher obligation rules: the obligation to save a friend.

In the end, your granddaughter will be relieved she sought you out. And in the future, she'll come to you with more problems.

There, don't you feel relieved, too?

The Unfavorite or "He's just harder to like."

My wife doesn't relate well to our nine-year-old grandson, Jason, adopted at age three. She is cordial to him, but she does quietly favor the two younger birth grandchildren.

Have you and your wife talked about this? Does she admit it or deny it? Does she acknowledge it, but downplay it?

Find a good time to talk. (Definitely not just after visiting the grandkids!) Start slow and easy. Ask some questions, seeking to understand, not correct. How is Jason different than his siblings? Is he less affectionate? More defiant? More aloof? Why do you think he's like that? What makes the younger kids easier to be around?

Focus on Jason, not your wife. Don't quibble with or dispute what you hear. Your goal is to hear it, allowing your wife to think out loud. Don't present the perspective that favoritism exists and that everybody can see it. The conversation could come to a fast halt.

There are several possible outcomes. Your wife may be ready to talk, aware that her partiality hasn't always been hidden. She may resist talking, especially if the adoption is at the root of her feelings. Feeling so is too ungrandmotherly. She could look perplexed, as if to say, "I don't get what you're saying." She could personalize, that is to say, "How could you think that of me?" Whatever her initial reaction, be patient. You don't have to resolve everything in one sit-down. Your questions planted seeds for thought. Future conversations are now more likely.

If you have your own struggles, admit them. You too sometimes have to work to connect with Jason. He doesn't seem as attached to you as the younger ones. Your struggles may surprise your wife, making it safer for her to admit hers. A "me too" revelation also shows her that you're not holding yourself up as her moral superior.

What if you don't struggle with Jason? Identify, then, someone with whom you do, preferably someone your wife knows. Your point is that not all personalities mesh easily. And sometimes, those personalities are in one's family.

Awareness of motives is a first step toward change. The next step is harder: change. As you accept your wife's feelings, remind her that they don't have to control her behavior, not consistently anyway. She may feel less warmth toward Jason, but she doesn't have to act with less warmth.

Encourage her to fake it, if need be, to act better than she feels. Small gestures—a hug, a hello, "How'd you do in your game?" or sitting by him as often as the other kids—will do much to show Jason his grandma likes him. More so than adults, children take another's behavior as it appears rather than looking for ulterior motives. If Grandma is acting nice, she must mean it.

Through it all, reassure your wife that she is not a "bad grandma." Jason may, in fact, be tougher to like, and that's OK. A good grandma is not one who never has negative emotions toward a grandchild; she is one who learns to control and act counter to those emotions.

Ancient philosophers advised, "Act well, and the feeling will follow." If Grandma acts well, both she and Jason will feel better.

Hyperactivated or "I can't keep up with all their activities."

As my grandchildren get older, they are involved in so many activities that I mostly see them when I'm a spectator. How can I fit into their lives more?

A paradox: The number of children per family is declining. The number of activities per child is increasing. A second paradox: Grandparents' schedules loosen. Grandkids' schedules tighten.

The word *hyperactive* describes more families these days. Go-go, move-move, do-do is a modern mantra. Lives are packed with practice, games, events, performances, and all the travel time to and from. One grandfather observed, "There's a lot less time to be bored together." Boredom enhances the stuff of relationships—listening, playing, giggling, hearing how little Grandpa had growing up and how much he appreciated it.

Perpetual motion lifestyles are an example of pursuing the good at the cost of the best. Sports, music, clubs—all provide positives for kids and their character. The challenge lies in maintaining balance between flurry and family, pace and peace. Little League ball for six-year-olds can be fun (if they are allowed to keep score), but draining when it involves two games a week (at approximately 3.2 hours each) and practice three other days.

Where does a grandparent fit into all this action? You identified one way: as a spectator. Absent the parents' epiphany that schedules are overpacked, for the meantime, flow with the schedule, though perhaps not all of it. Move alongside the pace at your own pace. You're not likely to persuade anyone to slow down. They have to figure that out on their own.

Still, there are eyes in the hurricane: the post action. Linger and orally replay the game or the event. Discuss performance. Ask the kids their assessment. Regale them with the time you scored six soccer goals in under four minutes.

"Did they have soccer when you were a kid, Grandpa?"

"Yes, but we had to kick rocks because nobody could afford a ball."

"Was the circle invented yet?"

Get a schedule of family activities. Where are the downsides? Insert yourself. Visit. Bring a movie. Invite anyone available to eat out—your treat.

Parents commonly express frustration at the frenzy. Here is your opening. Ask some questions to spur a parental awakening.

1) How often does everyone eat together, like we used to do? How much do conflicting schedules interfere with family time?

2) Do the kids routinely complain about being bored? (The irony: the faster we jam each minute, the quicker we're bored.)

3) When was the last time you went two days without some demand?

4) How often can both of you attend the same event, or are each of you at different places with different children?

I confess, I wrote this answer while sitting in the car, waiting for my nephew's game to start so I could catch a couple of innings before I had to be at my granddaughter's recital. Or was it during my grown son's intramural basketball game just before meeting my wife for our weekly book study?

Childhood Comparing or "When I was your age..."

When I tell my teen grandsons about my childhood and how different it was from theirs, after about two sentences, I lose them.

It all hit around age forty: I started sentences with, "When I was a boy..." As a grandfather, I start even more that way, coupled with some historical embellishment.

"When I was a boy, I walked over nine miles to school, in a foot of nuclear waste, with no shoes. We had one pair for seven kids, and my turn only came around once a week. And I always gave my turn away—that's the kind of boy I was. And I was grateful for what little I had."

"What did you have, Grandpa?"

"Nothing! But we were happy children."

As the saying goes, "The older we get, the greater we were." Comparing childhoods is a staple of life lectures for parents and grandparents alike. They are meant to instruct, foster gratitude, and broaden a youngster's perspective. All this while wrapped in oral swagger for what we endured and thrived through.

These are noble ends, but the means of getting there may fall on deaf ears. As little as our youth moved our own children, it moves our grandchildren even less. Two generations away, they see our childhood as a time when the earth was still cooling, and all we had to worry about was not being a T.rex's lunch.

What they don't realize is that someday, they too will compare childhoods. "When I was your age, we only had 550 channels on a TV that was two dimensional, and it only covered half the wall. We had to use these things called remotes, which you pushed with a finger. Sometimes we had to switch fingers if one got too sore." Just doesn't have the same oomph, does it?

Should you stifle all stories about your younger days? Not necessarily. Some kids are actually curious about the lived past. Give them the day-to-day details, unembellished. Speak matter-of-factly without saying, "You kids don't know how good you've got it." Tell also how you didn't feel deprived. This could shock them, as they know they'd feel deprived. To get and keep their attention longer, curtail any self-promotion or tone that says, "We were better kids—more respectful, hardworking, and more grateful." In our eyes, that may be true, but their eyes say, "Once upon a time, in a galaxy far, far away."

How long you linger on the past depends upon how well you read the present. Are the kids gazing off, texting, needing to go to the bathroom—again? If so, close quickly, "Well, I guess I did grow up a lot different than today."

As I age, I appreciate more the circumstances that helped shape me. And I'm more inclined to share them with the old and the young. I also have come to appreciate, however, that the young may not be the most receptive audience. Age will teach them a broader life perspective.

Anyway, that's how I see it, because when I was a boy...

Battered Parents or "Why do their parents allow such disrespect?"

My two grandsons are teenagers. Their disrespect to their parents shocks me. I don't know why they allow it. I never would have gotten away with talking to my parents that way.

There are two competing explanations. One, the parents hear the disrespect but don't discipline it. Two, they don't hear it anymore. In other words, they've grown deaf to snotty remarks and tone.

This latter explanation I've dubbed the Battered Parent Syndrome. It accounts for some of the difference between prior generations' mouth restraint and the present generation's mouth liberty.

Here's a scenario.

Diva (in a demanding tone): Mom, are you ready to go yet? I've got stuff I have to do at home. I've got to wash my hair and redo my nails.

Mom (in a placating tone): I know, honey. Just let me finish my coffee and we'll get going. Thanks for being patient. (Turning to Grandpa) She does have a lot to do.

Diva (definitely snarky): You said we'd leave twenty minutes ago. How much coffee are you going to have? If I'd have known this, I wouldn't have come.

Mom (trying to soothe Diva): OK, just give me a few more

minutes to talk with Grandpa about dinner Saturday, and then I'll say goodbye.

Diva (full snot mode): Just give me the keys. Give me the keys. I'll be in the car. Hurry up.

Diva is verbally blistering her mother while Mom is talking accommodation and singing "Kumbaya." Mom gives little indication of recognizing how she is being treated.

When a teen is accosting his parent in my office, I may ask, "Do you hear how's he's talking to you?" The reaction is stunned epiphany coupled with a look that says, "You're right. I am getting mistreated."

The parent doesn't challenge my observation. He is paying me for it, after all. Such might not be the case with you, a grandparent. Are you paid for your common sense?

To get a parent's attention, start nonverbally: a cringe. Your face makes a statement. To add emphasis, you can add an "Ouch!" You're noting the child's conduct rather than the parent's permissiveness.

If your cringe doesn't make the parent cringe, address your grandchildren. "Is that how you speak to your mother? Do you hear how you're talking to your father?" Of course, Butkus could answer, "Yes, it is," and "Yeah, I do." Should he be so brutally frank, he might shock the parents more than anything you could say.

Finally, when the timing is right, ask Mom or Dad, "Do you like what you're hearing?" or, "Don't you think you deserve more respect?" You're not waiting for an answer. You just want to spur thinking.

I wouldn't cringe or comment each time you hear disrespect and the parents don't. Your intent is not to point out parenting flaws. Your intent is to raise awareness. Note the irony: While Mom or Dad are oblivious to Noble's hurtful words, they may be oversensitive to your helpful ones.

Should you receive a "Don't tell me how to parent" reaction, say no more, now and in the future. To borrow some advice to mothers on their child's wedding day: Sit up, shut up, and wear beige. Do grandfathers even know what color that is? I don't.

The good news: Most parents over time become more aware they're being verbally battered, with or without a grandparent's input.

Rude Presence or "Talk nicer."

For years, my son and his wife have allowed disrespect and defiance, making the kids unpleasant to be around. I'll confess, I'm struggling to like them.

A tragedy of raising an undisciplined child is what it invites for the child. Others don't want to be around him, and those others sometimes are the child's own grandparents.

What you are describing doesn't sound like some transitory adolescent unruliness. "For years," you said, the parents have allowed defiance. When the kids were younger, it might have been easier to overlook, as they had the cuteness to counterbalance the rudeness. As teens, they've outgrown the cuteness. The rudeness is in the ascendancy.

Do you feel guilty about your struggle? Your reaction is understandable. The kids are difficult to be around. But aren't grandparents supposed to be extra tolerant? Tolerance doesn't mean abandoning your standards. Even if the kids' misconduct is not directed toward you, it is directed toward their parents, one of whom is your child. Parental protection instincts remain long after childrearing is past.

Being a grandparent can actually make it harder to control your feelings. You have a close interest in wanting your grandchildren to mature into likeable, pleasant people. And you're wrestling with doubts about when or if it will turn around.

What are your options? One, give your irritation a rest. That is, stretch the time between visits, not to punish children or parents, but to give yourself time to settle. Keeping your cool, and tongue, might come easier when you've had time to regroup.

If the parents notice your periodic absence, you can explain: "It's hard for me to watch how the kids treat you. You never treated me that way (if true). Sometimes they act rude toward me, too. I want to enjoy them when I do see them, so I put a little more time in between visits."

An honest confession and likely a shocker, how it's received depends upon how solid your relationship is with your son and his wife. If they've been defensive about the kids in the past, they may not understand your reaction. On the other hand, if they too are frustrated with the kids' conduct, you may give them the needed push to reverse course. They are seeing real-life consequences of allowing children to be obnoxious.

The second option is to accept what is: Your grandchildren are not giving you the relationship you had hoped for or anticipated. Eventually, that could change, but right now, lower your expectations and you'll lower your frustration. This doesn't mean that you approve of their behavior. It means recognizing what you can't control, which is their upbringing.

Are you bewildered over your children's raising their own children so unlike they themselves were raised? Are you wondering, "What happened?" Part of what happened is that parenting practices have changed. There has been a significant shift toward a less authoritative and looser disciplinary style, pushed hard by childrearing experts, who are uneasy with what was once considered firm, healthy discipline.

As a long-time (a nice way of saying "old") psychologist, I have worked with two generations of parents. I've watched the trend move away from "I'm the parent; you're not" and toward "Can't we all just cooperate now?" Cooperation is a good thing, but when it becomes the main discipline principle, it often leads to more uncooperative children. And grandparents are among the first to feel the effects up close and personal.

What about disrespect directed at you? Obviously, you don't have the discipline leverage of a parent. Still, you can comment: "That's a pretty snotty remark. Where did you learn that eye roll? Is that how you treat your grandfather (mother)?" Sometimes the least words say the most: "Ouch." The kids may not hear you, but their parents might.

A final option. Master the blank, dumfounded look, which says, "I don't understand what's happening here. Why is this allowed?" Blank looks speak clearly. And they don't risk an argument because you didn't say a word.

Please Say Thank You or "Whatever happened to common courtesy?"

Good manners were expected from us as children. My older grandchildren seldom use them. Do I remind them?

Please, thank you, yes sir, no ma'am, excuse me. A small handful of words, mostly one or two syllables, speak volumes. More than social protocol, manners afford respect. They say, in few words, "I will treat you with courtesy because I believe you deserve it."

Granted, the average little kid isn't pondering this meaning with his "thank you." He is just reiterating how he's been told to talk. Even so, a habit of good character is being rooted. Time will add meaning.

Sloppiness with manners is part of an overall social trend toward informality. Mr. and Mrs. yield to first names when young address old. Clothing styles weave themselves toward "whatever." Look at sixty-year-old pictures of large crowds—sporting events, amusement parks, church. Suits dominate among men, Sunday best among women. Now, sartorial cool is defined as pretorn jeans and baggy sweatshirts. It follows that our language has become, I mean, you know, like looser and stuff.

Still, parents strive to teach manners, at least in the early years. They nudge hundreds of times—thousands?—before a child turns six, "What do you say? How do you ask nicely? What's the magic word?" When nudges fail, they get direct: "Say 'thank you.'" They recognize that this practice is socially worthwhile.

Most people extrapolate positive personality traits from

manners—respect, kindness, maturity. And they reciprocate with compliments ("How polite"), admiration ("Isn't she sweet?"), and tangibles ("Can I give him another cookie?").

As you observe, your generation grew up with more emphasis on manners. What you were taught you taught your children. You expected your children to teach theirs. And they probably did, more so when their children were younger but less so as they got older. They lost manners momentum.

With preschoolers, courteous words have a sound and feel of novelty, along with prompting accolades and cookies. With teens, a sort of linguistic inertia settles in. It takes more effort to be polite. What's more, it's not all that cool. It smacks of an Eddie Haskell persona. Since this book is for grandparents, I'm assuming most of you remember Eddie.

Is it time to begin a Manners 101 reeducation program? Do you remind your family as you did twenty or more years ago? Where do you start? Parents, or kids, or both? Speaking to the parents alone is risky. You could be heard as critical or opinionated. Besides, how many times would you have to remind them? The more you repeat yourself, the less you're heard. Just like when they were kids.

There is a way to teach adult and child simultaneously. Wait for Grace to display manners to you or her parents. Hopefully before she's married. Then compliment. "Politeness makes you sound mature. Well, thank you, too. Your mom (dad) was very polite as a child; you're like that." When all else fails, try, "Want a cookie?"

It's been said, "We don't so much act according to how others see us, but more how we think they see us." If Mom or Dad think you think the kids are mannerly, they may act to make the kids more mannerly.

Teach your grandkids using the same principle you used decades ago with their parents. Nothing is given without a "please;" nothing is to be received without a "thank you." You don't need to prompt, "What do you say?" or "Is that how you ask?" A simple blank look will convey, "I'm waiting for the right words."

Thank you for listening. Please buy this book for all the grandparents you know.

Vanishing Adolescents or "Where did all my grandkids go?"

My grandchildren are twelve and fourteen years old. When they were younger, they loved spending time with my wife and me. In the past few years, we've seen less and less of them. They always seem to have something else to do or somewhere else to go.

Once upon a time, with age came respect. Several decades of life brought knowledge and experience. The old were a valued source of wisdom for the young, who hung around them to absorb some of it.

Today's culture reveres youth. What matters most is beauty, vigor, coolness (whatever that means). A mindset is: The older one is, the less in touch he is with the latest trend. And few ages are more consumed with the latest trends than teens. As I heard one say, "That is so last week."

Many experts intone: It is normal and healthy for adolescents to separate from adults, seeking autonomy in the pursuit of self-identification—or some such psychoverbiage. I'll bet their grandkids don't hang around with them either.

Certainly age-related independence evolves. A fourteen-year-old has more social options than an eight-year-old and a whole lot more than a three-year-old. It seems, though, that too many options are coming too soon.

The adolescent drift away from us older folks—which includes parents, who in kid eyes are also older folks—is as much due to modern society as to development, if not more so. As the typical youngster's life has become more go-go, get-get, do-do, the competition for family time has expanded exponentially.

I mean, why would Chase head to Grandma's when he can stay home, tally 112 likes on social media, peruse 172 TV channels, and then get picked up by Freeman, whose house comes equipped with 452 channels, virtual reality games, and a cute sister who also didn't go with her family to visit Grandma and Grandpa.

Most likely, your grandchildren still like being with you. It's just that the lure to be elsewhere is stronger. As their option list lengthens, their former top-ten pick—time with Grandma and Grandpa—slips to number twenty-two.

How can you climb the list? Some grandparents are direct, with a little guilt sprinkled in. "It's been quite a while since we've seen you. Are you leaving already? So when will we see you again?" One grandmother went with all-out guilt. Upon seeing the kids, she greeted them with, "And your name is?"

This recalls the joke about the son who phones his mother and hears a weak-sounding, "Hello."

"Mom, you sound awful. What's going on?"

"I haven't eaten in sixteen days."

"That's terrible. Why?"

"I didn't want my mouth to be full of food in case you called."

Guilt is a form of persuasion that doesn't work too well with any age. It may prod some cooperation, but it's better if kid visits are free rather than obligatory.

Do you then have to accept what you get, content to reminisce about the old days filled with more grandchildren? Fortunately, as they have options, so do you. As they show less initiative, you show more. Extend more invites—movies, ball games, eating out, social events, bingo. Ok, maybe scratch the bingo. The kids won't go, unless you promise to share your prize money.

Would you become a goodie-giving grandparent? That depends upon the goodie. Is it a new video game per week at your house? A monthly cruise? A week-long red Corvette rental? These might be considered forms of visitation bribery. On the other hand, the day-to-day stuff of family get-togethers can all be the focal points of really old stuff, like you know, talking to each other, joking, and playing.

Parents are the key to reversing the vanishing adolescent trend. As long as they allow Liberty to independently choose where to go and what to do, it's no surprise that he does so. They may wish for more of his presence, but they're reluctant to push it. Let them know, in neither a complaining or accusatory tone, how much you enjoy the kids, especially as they're getting older. At first, they may offer some feeble rationales: "She's studying for the college ACT four years early. I think he's feeling the need to spend more quality time with his younger sister." Believe it or not, some parents badly underestimate how much the grandparents miss seeing the kids. You can remind them.

Children regularly have to be made to act in their own long-term interests. (Who doesn't?) Throughout my teen years, I regularly visited Momo and Popo—my grandparents. It was an unspoken nonnegotiable. That wasn't the only reason I went, though. One, I loved them. Two, there were few digital distractions then to swallow my time. And three, my grandmother fed me the instant I got out of the car, ceasing only as I walked out the door with bags of grub in each arm. Number three was a big draw for a teenage boy. How well do you cook?

My grandfather's sister, Aunt Mary, was in her nineties. She was frail, hard of hearing, and kept her thermostat way too high for my comfort. My mother asked me to accompany her on visits to Aunt Mary's, but they weren't really requests. Left to me, I could concoct all kinds of alternatives. Over time, just by sitting at my aunt's table, hearing about her younger life and her asking me about mine, I absorbed some of the wisdom of her age. In the end, she gave me more than I gave her, even if I didn't realize that until years later.

When all else fails, you could try some subtlety. Ask Mom or Dad. "So, how are the kids doing these days? I bet they're getting big."

The Tech Zone or "Put down your phone and talk."

When my teen grandchildren visit, their noses are stuck in their cell phones or other devices.

Cutting-edge communication cuts two ways. It can connect families divided by distance, delivering a personal touch not possible one generation ago. It can disconnect families who do live near each other, interfering with the personal touch.

It comes down to mathematics: the more time spent in the tech zone, the less time spent in the people zone. What's more, it is the young among us that are most drawn to the tech zone, too often with parental assent, leaving the older among us feeling the impersonal effects.

Speak first with your grandchildren. Emphasize how much you enjoy their company. How much you want to hear all about school, activities, friends, and if you're anything like my Italian mother, how much you enjoy feeding them. Whether you ask them outright to limit their non-face time is your call. They may hear what you're saying and self-disconnect. If not, try some cannoli.

Next, if need be, approach Mom and Dad. Reinforce your pleasure over the family visits and hearing from the kids about their lives. Explain how be much easier it would be to connect with the kids if they were less connected to their phones. Avoid a scolding tone. It will get you disconnected. After all, if the parents allow Alexander and Belle unlimited tech time, they could hear you questioning their judgment. Worse, they could think you're stuck in the old days, like 1987, unaware that, "that's just how kids interact nowadays."

If the face-to-face is unsuccessful, try an email, along with an Instagram picture of the kids glued to their phones. A YouTube video probably would be overkill.

You could suggest a rule similar to that of one mother I talked to. When visiting anyone, all cell phones are to be placed in silent mode and deposited on the counter for the entire stay.

I asked, "Yours, too?"

She replied, "Yes, but it's tough."

Her grandchildren aren't even teenagers yet.

Another grandmother made this observation about the Pavlovian power of a cell phone's beckoning: "When I'm with someone whose cell phone sounds, if she tries to ignore it, she looks like she's almost in pain. It's as though she's thinking, 'Let me see if this is someone more important than you.'"

We older folks didn't grow up with all this relentless clamoring for our attention. Our alternatives for person-to-person contact were other person-to-person contacts. Though we may not relate to the allure of the tech zone, we needn't surrender our closest relationships to it. Speak up, in person, to whomever might listen.

Or, put all the kids' numbers in your phone's contact list. Then send out a group text asking for some face-to-face time.

Differing Views or "I don't think it will hurt them."

I allow my grandsons, ages ten and twelve, to watch television shows at my house that their parents don't approve of. I think they're a little too tight on their viewing rules, and I don't see how some of what I allow is going to hurt the boys.

"It's not going to hurt them" is one of a group of related arguments: "It's not like they're going to go out and assault somebody. They're only seeing what real life is like; they'll have to see it eventually." And the oft repeated: "You can't shelter them forever."

No doubt, you believe your grandsons are pretty good kids. As such, they can digest some visual bile and stomach it. Their morals are solid enough that the tube's immorality "won't hurt them."

In teaching character, the question is not: What harm will it do? The question is: What good will it do? Humans can survive all manner of threats and assaults, to body and soul. That doesn't mean they are beneficial. The body can defeat all kinds of life-endangering germs. Are these germs then of no menace?

At age fourteen, while carrying four folding chairs under my arms, I fell face-first down twelve steps onto a concrete floor (I think I was executing my sister's double-dog dare.) Except for a bruised ego, I walked away unscathed. I shudder to think how my body would respond now. Did this mean I should attempt a flying Wallenda again sometime? After all, it didn't hurt me.

Grandparents have a range of motives for offering more channels than a parent. "It won't hurt them" ranks number one. "Balancing the scale" is also on the list. If a grandparent thinks the parents are too far outside cultural norms, they may try to compensate with added freedoms where they can. If the parents are too strict in their view, Grandma or Grandpa can provide some looseness. I mean, most other kids their age know what's popular in the media. Shouldn't they? The risk here lies in broadcasting an unspoken message to the children: "Your parents are too tight on their TV rules; I'll correct it when you're with me." Consequently, the kids would naturally see Grandpa as the more TV savvy grown-up, an attitude that could be broadcast back home.

A third motive is contrasting visions. Today's parents are distressed over the video sewage beamed incessantly at their children, forcing them to protect and supervise. Grandparents who lived during a morally safer TV era may underestimate the amount and effect of the cinematic assaults aimed at a child's well-being. We've come a long way fast from Mayberry to South Park.

A fourth motive is likeability. Grandparents like being liked by the grandkids. And indeed, it's easier for us to be. We don't typically have to set the boundaries that parents do. We have extra leeway in fulfilling wishes. So, we might permit a small amount of visual ugliness in exchange for Emmy's being happy with us during our mutual viewing time.

Let's assume that, in fact, it won't hurt them, that Mom and

Dad's rules could use a little relaxing, and that the boys will see Grandpa as more kid-friendly. All of which is irrelevant. The overarching consideration is respect for parents' viewer ratings. You don't need to agree; just cooperate.

Fight the urge to form any sort of conspiracy with the boys. "You can't watch this at home, but it's okay here. Just keep it between us."

First, that's undercutting Mom and Dad. Almost never does any good come out of that for anyone. Second, conspiracies are almost always exposed in some way. Even if Nielson and Oscar don't tattle, their conduct at home could. They might replay what they've seen or use words foreign to their house but native to TV. It's a rare child who doesn't somehow reflect, in language, behavior, or attitude, what they have absorbed with their eyes.

A strong viewer warning: Don't force the parents to pull the plug. That is, refusing to cooperate with them may push them to take dramatic action: No more alone time with Grandpa. All visits will now be in the company of a parent. And no overnighters. No television program is worth those conditions.

It rates a rerun: Your views as grandparent must yield to their views as parents. Is the picture clear?

TV or Not TV or "Most kids have one."

I bought my twelve-year-old grandson a television for his bedroom. I've since found out that his parents have not allowed him to have it. Don't I have a right to give a gift?

That depends. What's the gift? A wall poster of the rock bad boys Felons in Chains? A subscription to *School Cheaters Today*? A ten-pound bag of chocolates?

The right to give any gift to a child not one's own rests upon two basics: (1) the appropriateness of the gift and (2) the parent's wishes.

A television, granted, is neither illegal nor immoral nor fattening. What it streams into your grandson's bedroom, however, could very well be all three. No doubt, this is where your gift clashed with his parents' wishes.

Your grandson likely has no television in his bedroom. Otherwise, why buy him one? Unless his current TV is outdated, sporting only a forty-six-inch screen. As an aside, the majority of teens' bedrooms house televisions. Your grandson is in a shrinking minority.

A grandparent may have the means and motive to give something the parents don't or won't. He could be moved by generational generosity or by wanting to grant a wish the parents haven't or by wanting to compensate a child he sees as shortchanged.

After all, most other kids his age have one; he is among the few who don't.

A grandparent may reason: I paid for it. He really wants it. Mom's overreacting. There's nothing wrong with it. He deserves it—he's a good kid.

Even if all these were true, whether to accept or decline any gift from anyone is squarely within a parent's prerogative. A mom told me how a gift caused a rift in her family. Grandma bought her fourteen-year-old son a TV for his room. Mom strongly disapproved, but Grandma warned, "I gave it to him, it's his, and if you refuse it, you will deal with me."

Mom was torn. On one hand, the thought of unsupervised TV deeply unsettled her. On the other, Grandma's threat portended a major family fracture. She asked me about her predicament.

I asked her, "If a classmate gave your son a bag of marijuana, would you confiscate it?"

"Absolutely," she said.

"Why?"

"Because it's not good for him."

"Then you've answered your own question. Your right to protect supersedes another's right to give, even if the giver is a close family member."

Suppose that you purchase for your grandson the latest basketball video game. In your eyes, a wholesome offering—no violence or sexual content, just pure entertainment. Suppose, too, the video game stays unopened for weeks, as your grandson breathlessly informs you every time he sees you. Lately he's even taken to wearing a sandwich board, "32 days without Grandpa's game."

What are his parents thinking? How can they question this? Perhaps they've had experience with their son's bonding to these types of games, and they don't want to battle over them. Perhaps they anticipate that his attachment to the tech world will crowd out schoolwork and chores. Perhaps they simply want him to do more reading, playing outside, and talking to Mom and Dad. Whatever their reasons—some you may think legitimate, others not—they know their son, and they know their goals for his character.

When our children were small, my wife and I put a limit on stuffed animals: one per child. I'll confess, sometimes we slipped to two or three. Our last child has 251—kidding, only fourteen. If one per child sounds extreme, consider that with ten young children, that's ten animals, the stuffed type, not the kids. Two apiece is twenty. Five apiece...well, you get the math.

No doubt, few parents, and even fewer grandparents, would put such a low ceiling on a stuffed playmate menagerie. Parenting, however, is not poll driven. Our reasons? One, to nudge the kids toward material moderation. Two, to teach appreciation for possessions. Three, to keep our home semi-litter free.

Our plan unfolded somewhat acceptably for a few years until our daughter, Hannah, at around age eight, started to tattle, "It's no use giving us this, Grandma, we probably can't keep it." Not totally true. Hannah still had her pick of which one to keep.

When giving a gift, particularly one that touches upon character or morals—candy and socks are pretty safe—you're smart to first run it by the parents. No matter what you think of their stance, don't dispute it. Accept it. Accept, too, that they likely aren't moved by ingratitude but by any number of other considerations, some of which you may not be aware of.

By the way, do you even have a television in your own bedroom? I don't.

The Journey Home or "We've opened up our home. For how long, I don't know."

My daughter was fired from her job a few months ago, and she and her son moved in with us. She's not been the most responsible young person, and she's making few moves toward independence. I want to set clear conditions, but if she then leaves, I worry for the well-being of my grandson.

It's a growing trend: adult children with children moving in with their parents, moving the parents to help out, bail out, or ultimately kick out.

Helping out. Having the resources, the grandparent(s) willingly offer their home. It's an enjoyable echo of earlier family life. The young adults are cooperative and have solid plans for independence. It's a preferable interim arrangement for all.

Bailing out. Unfortunate circumstances (job loss, breakups, financial troubles) push the adult back to Mom and Dad's. Sometimes a good option; sometimes the only option. The grandparents then step in to reduce the pressure, at times with mixed feelings, more so if any previous move-backs didn't go so well. Nonetheless, out of love, obligation, or concern for a grandchild, the doors are open in the hope that this transition will go smoothly.

Kicking out. An unhappy ending. While the household blend may have begun agreeably, with conditions acceptable to all, over time, the adult child becomes more settled, and her parents less so. She shows less cooperation, initiative, and recognition of whose house it is. Her conduct is reminiscent of her adolescence. This sounds like your situation.

Compounding the strain are disagreements between grandparents. One wants to set limits; the other is reluctant. One wants to set a timetable; the other resists. At the center of this discord is the worry: "What about our grandchild? He needs the benefits of being here."

Life doesn't always present clear-cut options: one good, one bad. Sometimes, both are bad, with one being less bad than the other. That seems to describe your dilemma.

Option one: Take a stand, set a timetable. Your daughter will at some point leave, voluntarily or involuntarily, taking her son with her. At times, the grandchild remains with the grandparents, but that is uncommon.

What's next? First, do all you can to avoid being estranged. Emphasize to your daughter that you still very much want to be part of her and her son's lives. You'll help however you can— babysitting, transportation, job hunting. Be careful about the financial aid you provide. It has the most potential for abuse.

No matter how accommodating you are, your daughter may still try to punish you by limiting or eliminating your contact with your grandson. In other words, "If you don't want me, then you don't want him."

Often, this is a knee-jerk emotional reaction. Heated emotions cool. Practicalities reassert themselves. Your daughter may come to realize that she still needs your support, whether she lives with you or not. And that her son still needs his grandparents.

Option two: Continue to live as you are, allowing your daughter to live as she is. Don't argue, nag, prod, persuade. You've decided to let her stay on her terms, so however possible, avoid verbal battles.

Couldn't she just grow that much more comfortable? Perhaps, but what have your words gained so far other than more resistance and multiplying excuses? Option two is primarily for your grandson's benefit. It allows him to be in your life daily. You accept your daughter's irresponsibility to give your grandson stability. It's a trade-off.

Consider the unknown part of option two: How long can you endure? Most grandparents do reach their limit before the child decides to move on and move ahead. Either swelling frustration takes its toll, or the young adult engages in completely intolerable behavior. Then, option one is forced: It's time to go.

One thought nags a grandparent at this outcome: If I could have persevered a little longer, maybe I'd have seen progress. Maybe I acted too soon.

More often than not, excessive toleration doesn't improve matters, it makes them worse. The live-in lifestyle becomes more entrenched, more entitled. Consequently, when the grandparent does finally take the stand that she's tried to avoid for so long, the rancor has been building. The ill will has reached a crescendo. The more ill will, the more likely the parent will separate the grandchild from the grandparents, no matter where she ends up living.

Here are two pieces of reassurance, whichever option you choose. One, because things didn't work out doesn't mean you were wrong to open your home. You acted in good faith, hoping for the best. Two, any ugly repercussions probably won't be permanent. For different reasons, your daughter and her son will likely see the benefits of supportive grandparents.

Second Time Around Childrearing or "I'm raising kids again."

Due to my son's family turmoil, we were granted custody of our grandchildren, ages seven and eleven. We're a little unsure of ourselves in this unexpected role as parents again.

Surveys tell of the growing numbers of grandparents raising grandchildren. The conditions are diverse. Are parents still part of the children's lives? Is there visitation—open or supervised? Were the grandparents close to the children prior to the new arrangement? Is custody temporary or permanent? Was it given up voluntarily or court-ordered? Some general themes, however, would apply to most circumstances.

Speak no evil. Be slow to criticize the parents. As turbulent as their former home life was, as irresponsible as their parents might have been, as erratic as their upbringing has been, most kids retain a sense of loyalty to their parents, as well as distress over their family's fracture. What ugly particulars you know that they don't, keep to yourself. They know enough and have already lived too much of it. Before revealing something, ask yourself, "What purpose will this serve?"

Don't correct the record. The urge to do so swells from two motives: (1) to protect the children and (2) to protect yourself. They did nothing to cause this outcome, despite what a parent might have told them. Since they deserve no blame, it's tempting to point to where the real blame lies—with one parent or both. It's a balancing act to reassure the kids without demeaning the parents. Correct where you need to, but spare unnecessary details. The parent(s) may have disparaged you, little or lots, so the impulse is strong to defend yourself to the kids. Clarify wherever needed, mainly to show that Grandpa and Grandma aren't so bad as they were portrayed. Give just enough perspective, preferring generalities, to give an accurate picture and to temper any resentments the kids might have formed through false portrayals.

Compensation. Feeling sorry for the kids is natural. They've had a hard life so far, so it's time to give them a softer one. If that means more love, more stability, better discipline, and healthier expectations, compensate away. If these were once lacking for the kids, they need them now more than ever.

If compensation means less discipline, less responsibility, and more possessions, that won't make up for a bad past. It just complicates the present. However well-intended, an attitude of, "They've had it so badly, I need to show more tolerance for bad behavior," almost always continues the past's troubles, only in different form.

Advice overload. Because your circumstances, though more common, are still not the norm, others' opinions on how you should be doing things may be plentiful. Their net effect could provoke uncertainty and second-guessing—neither of which will help you help the kids. You are the final word. Sort through the advice (including mine) to judge what will work best for your new family, when and how. As one grandfather responded to critical opinions, "I like the way I'm doing it better than the way you're not."

Parent first, grandparent second. An adult child has made you a grandparent. Circumstances have made you a second-time-around parent. To be a good grandparent, be a good parent first. Setting expectations, rules, and supervision are now part of your primary calling. You are not a default parent thrust into the role by unforeseen complications. You have all the rights and responsibilities of a parent. The perks of grandparenthood—a relaxed relationship, healthy generosity, extra free time—can still be enjoyed, but only in the context of being a strong, confident big person.

After their years of being a parent-grandparent, many look back and think, "I don't know who benefitted more—me or the kids."

Using Children to Punish or "I'm not allowed to see my grandchildren."

I'm a grandmother who got off on the wrong foot with my daughter-in-law. Over time, our relationship has just gotten worse. Recently she's been finding excuses to keep our young grandchildren away from us.

Whose foot was it? Would you answer hers, and she yours? Or do both of you have a leg in this?

Here's a standard progression, or as it were, regression. Early contacts are neither easy nor warm. You find things hard to accept about her, likewise, she about you. Opinions collide, slights build, feelings bruise, motives are misread. The attitude evolves, "We find each other harder to like. Let's just stay cordial."

The dynamic isn't always limited to the two adults at its center. Other family members regularly get pulled in. In addition to seeing less of your grandchildren, are you seeing less of your son? The downward spiral seems persistent. Fortunately, it isn't.

The first step in mending a relationship begins with the self, more specifically with self-scrutiny, the willingness to analyze oneself. What can you find in you that could be contributing to the friction? Need help in the search? Ask your spouse. Then listen, don't defend. Self-scrutiny is neither easy nor pleasant. The human inclination is to resist looking inward for flaws. Looking outward at others is more natural. Through my eyes, the problem is you, not me.

"My mother-in-law is intrusive," so declares daughter-in-law. Meaning, she inserts herself unasked and uninvited into their family's affairs. There are edgy tones, unsought childrearing advice, manipulation. Whether Grandma's opinions are accurate or not is not the main consideration. Because one is right doesn't mean she'll be heard. It's been said: "If you want to make me mad, tell a lie about me. If you want to make me really mad, tell the truth about me." Before speaking your truth, ask yourself, "Will this smooth or wrinkle our relationship?"

Have you been in any way intrusive? If you're like most of us, the times we can recall are a fraction of the total, due mostly to memory fading and self-defense, "I didn't mean anything by it." Apply a power of ten rule. Multiply the times you do remember by ten to get a more accurate count.

My intent is not to impugn your honest attempts to get along, nor to place a large share of blame at your feet. It is to move you to discern how you can better the relationship, independent of your daughter-in-law's efforts.

"I honestly don't think it's me. She has been difficult since she started dating my son." If so, that means it's even more urgent to watch yourself. If she is overly sensitive or insecure or prone to take offense, know that any remark, however it is meant to be helpful or corrective, could be misinterpreted. What you might say to your son without repercussion you can't say to his wife.

"Then, I guess I just have to walk on eggs around her." No, you just have to keep most opinions to yourself. Concluding she's more to blame for this wrong-footed dance won't help you see more of your grandkids. And that is your ultimate aim.

"I don't understand why my son doesn't do anything about this." He may have tried, but two realities may be asserting themselves. One, he mostly hears his wife's side. Hearing her upset regularly can shape his perspective. Two, it behooves him to keep peace in his marriage. He could want to speak up in your defense, but he knows he'll cause marital tension. Put simply, don't take his silence or passivity personally.

Now for damage control. Suppose after some healthy self-scrutiny, you realize that you indeed have said or done things that could be considered intrusive. (Did you sit up, shut up, and wear beige on her wedding day?)

Approach your daughter-in-law by saying, "I am so sorry that I have stuck my nose where it doesn't belong. It's none of my business how you and my son run your family, and I'm asking your forgiveness. I promise, I will work hard not to be like that anymore." However you wish to say it, what matters most are sincerity and no excuses.

"I really don't think I've done anything wrong." Two responses. One, it is a rare individual who can't legitimately find anything to self-correct in a relationship, however small her share. Two, if your daughter-in-law is prone to misconceptions, in apologizing, you are giving some of her perceptions credibility. That can be most humbling.

Halfway through your expression of contrition, your daughter-in-law may faint. Or she may stare back, as if to say, "yeah, right." ("See, I told you she was difficult!") Nevertheless, your intent is to regroup, showing her over time that your resolve is solid. While you may never become the best of friends, the tension should ease. And that should open up more opportunities to spend time with your grandkids.

Unplanned Grandparenthood or "This isn't how I thought I'd first be a grandparent."

I have several grandchildren, some born in a marriage, some not. It isn't exactly how I expected to be a grandparent.

Two generations ago, the out-of-wedlock birth rate hovered between 5 and 10 percent for many generations. Currently it is passing 40 percent, with widespread repercussions for society and for grandparents. Many grandparents are watching grandchildren being born and raised outside a two-parent marriage. As one grandfather wryly observed, "I'm hoping for an equal number of in-wedlock and out-of-wedlock grandchildren."

A range of permutations result: single moms, live-in fathers, live-in boyfriends, disappearing dads, half-siblings, maybe marriages, grandparents as parents. All leaving grandparents to watch and wonder: What is my role? How should I be involved? How much help do I give—financial, housing, emotional? This isn't what they thought grandparenting would look like. They had anticipated a more traditional, indeed smoother, stage of life. Through all the uncertainties, however, most grandparents recognize one constant: The child is innocent. Whatever the choices and circumstances of his parents, none of it is his doing.

Situation one: The mother is your daughter. However hurt and disappointed you might feel as her parent, to the extent possible, don't pull away. The more erratic her lifestyle, the more tempting a retreat for her might be. Estrangement is the enemy. It will eliminate any positive influence you could have. You may just have to put more energy into keeping a connection with your daughter and her child, though that might not come as easily or naturally as with any other grandchildren.

The future is not here yet. (Am I profound or what?) You can't know how things will unfold. Will your daughter marry? And who—the child's father or someone else? Will she move far away or nearby, or move in with you? Will you be raising your grandchild? Circumstances will fluctuate. What they are presently may not at all be what they will be in one, two, or five years from now. Your role may take some twists and turns.

Situation two: the father is your son. The best-case scenario is that he invites your presence in the child's life. He and the mother are still together, with marriage a possibility someday. Take advantage of any openings to help, but be cautious about giving opinions or advice to your son or the mother unless they are clearly sought. In short, give guidance only when asked. Your role is vulnerable to shifts in their relationship, so you're wise to step gingerly.

Don't send signals that you don't like the mother, are only tolerating her, or wishing that your son wasn't with her. All these emotions may be present, but expressing them could push her away from you, taking along your grandson and even your son. To use gaming language, she holds all the cards. Work within the hand you've been dealt.

Situation three: the mother is not emotionally involved with your son or he with her. This is by far the most unpredictable scenario. If the mother of your grandchild has little or no contact with your son, then you too are likely going to be out of the picture. Most grandparents isolated in this way find support through prayers. They are forced to accept only what the mother allows, which may be minimal, if at all.

Perhaps your son is creating the distance; he wants no contact or responsibility for the child. Some birth moms may welcome your support independent of your son. Your connection with her could provide a bridge for your son should he ever have a change of heart. Again, the future isn't here yet.

Situation four: You become both parent and grandparent. Most often, this is through a daughter's child, less so for a son's. Sometimes daughter lives with parents; sometimes because of neglect or chaos, grandparents gain legal custody. Since this outcome is detailed elsewhere in this book, I won't revisit it here.

The common denominator in all these scenarios is complications—familial and emotional, foreseen or unexpected. Finding yourself in any one of them can test you to the limits of your endurance. Still, someone has to be the stable, mature adult, and you're selected.

ADDITIONAL RESOURCES FOR GRANDPARENTS
from Franciscan Media

Find these and more at
shop.franciscanmedia.org or in your favorite bookstore

. . . .

True Radiance

Finding Grace in the Second Half of Life

BY LISA MLADNICH

Discover the beauty that comes with faith and a life lived well.

. . . .

101 Places to Pray Before You Die

A Roamin' Catholic's Guide

BY THOMAS J. CRAUGHWELL

Add some prayer to your next family vacation.

Eight Whopping Lies and Other Stories of Bruised Grace

BY BRIAN DOYLE

Reflect on family, love, and faith with this book of short personal essays.

At Play in God's Creation

An Illuminating Coloring Book

BY TARA M. OWENS AND DANIEL SORENSEN

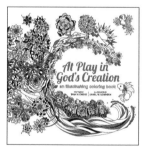

Pray, create, and color together as a family.

The Chime Travelers series

BY LISA M. HENDEY

Give young readers the gift of an encounter with the saints.

ABOUT THE AUTHOR

Dr. Ray Guarendi is a clinical psychologist, prolific author and speaker, and nationally syndicated radio host. His radio show, The Doctor Is In, can be heard weekdays on EWTN, Ave Maria Radio, and Sirius XM. His many books include *Discipline That Lasts a Lifetime*, *You're a Better Parent Than You Think*, and *Winning the Discipline Debates*. He and his wife are the parents of ten children.